Yorkshire
A Very Peculiar History

"See all, hear all, say nowt,
Eat up, sup up, pay nowt,
An if tha does owt for nowt
Allus do it for thysen."

Yorkshire proverb, 'The Tyke's Motto'

First published in the UK in 2011
by The Salariya Book Company Ltd
Originally created and designed by David Salariya
This edition published in the UK in 2025 by Hatch Press,
an imprint of Bonnier Books UK
5th Floor, HYLO, 105 Bunhill Row
London, EC1Y 8LZ

Copyright ©2025 by Hatch Press

3 5 7 9 10 8 6 4 2

All rights reserved

ISBN 978-1-83527-113-3

Printed in China

The authorised representative in the EEA is
Bonnier Books UK (Ireland) Limited.
Registered office address:
Block B, The Crescent Building
Northwood, Santry
Dublin 9, D09 C6X8, Ireland
compliance@bonnierbooks.ie

Yorkshire
A Very Peculiar History

Written by
John Malam

Hatch

"Everything they think soon gets to the tongue, and out it comes, heads and tails, as fast as they can pour it."

William Cobbett, 1830, describing the outspoken nature of Yorkshire folk

"My living in Yorkshire was so far out of the way that it was actually twelve miles from a lemon."

Sydney Smith, 1855, vicar at Foston-le-Clay, grumbling about having to travel to York, the nearest big town

"I've never found a Yorkshire accent a disadvantage. A Yorkshire accent is taken as a mark of having lived in the real world."

Sir Bernard Ingham, 1999, Yorkshireman and civil servant

"Yorkshire born and Yorkshire bred, strong in the arm and weak in the head."

Yorkshire proverb

Contents

Putting Yorkshire on the map	6
Introduction: Where the 'eck is Yorkshire?	9
1 Prehistoric Yorkshire	15
2 Roman Yorkshire	29
3 Between the Romans and the Vikings	41
4 Viking Yorkshire	49
5 Norman Yorkshire	61
6 Castles and cathedrals	73
7 Poor peasants and mean monks	87
8 The bloody roses	103
9 Oi, Henry! Hands off!	119
10 Rebels, Royalists & Roundheads!	131
11 Made in Yorkshire and proud of it!	147
12 Yorkshire factfile	163
Acknowledgements	181
Glossary	182
Timeline of Yorkshire history	184
Index	188

Putting Yorkshire on the map
A map of Yorkshire showing pre-1974 boundaries of the Ridings and significant towns and cities.

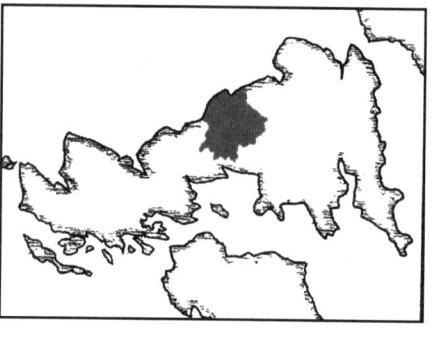

✗ = Battle site

- - - = Ridings border

1. York
2. Doncaster
3. Scarborough
4. Bradford
5. Leeds
6. Huddersfield
7. Halifax
8. Barnsley
9. Wakefield
10. Knaresborough
11. Hull
12. Beverley
13. Rotherham
14. Sheffield
15. Harrogate

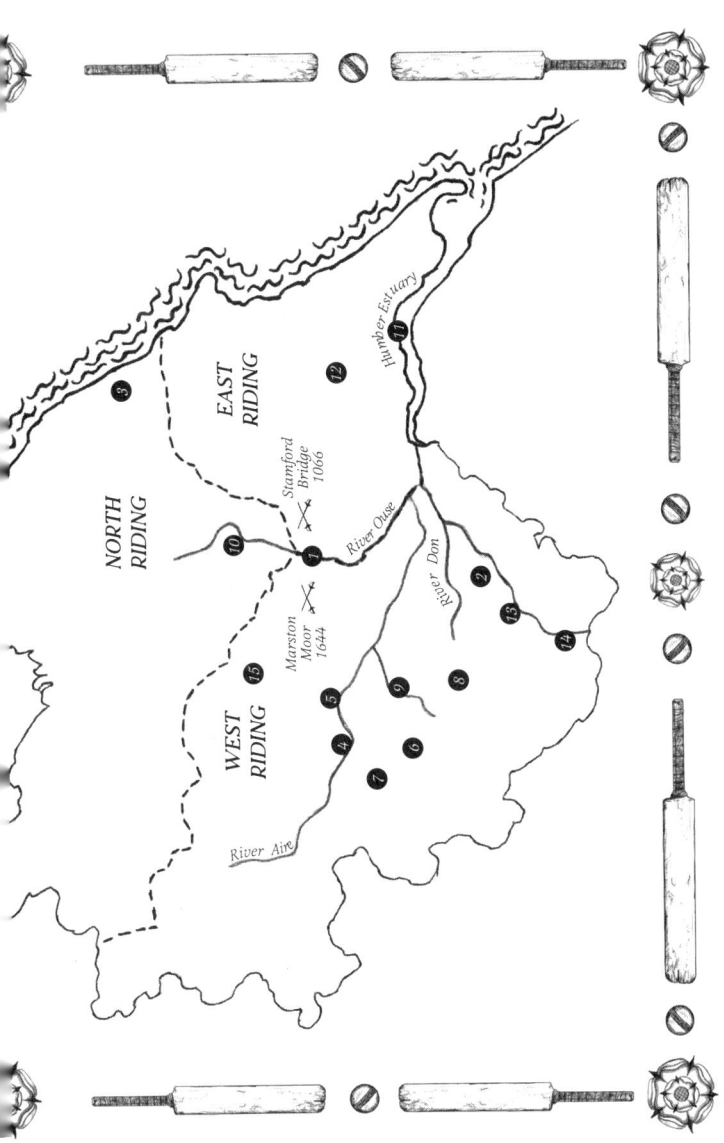

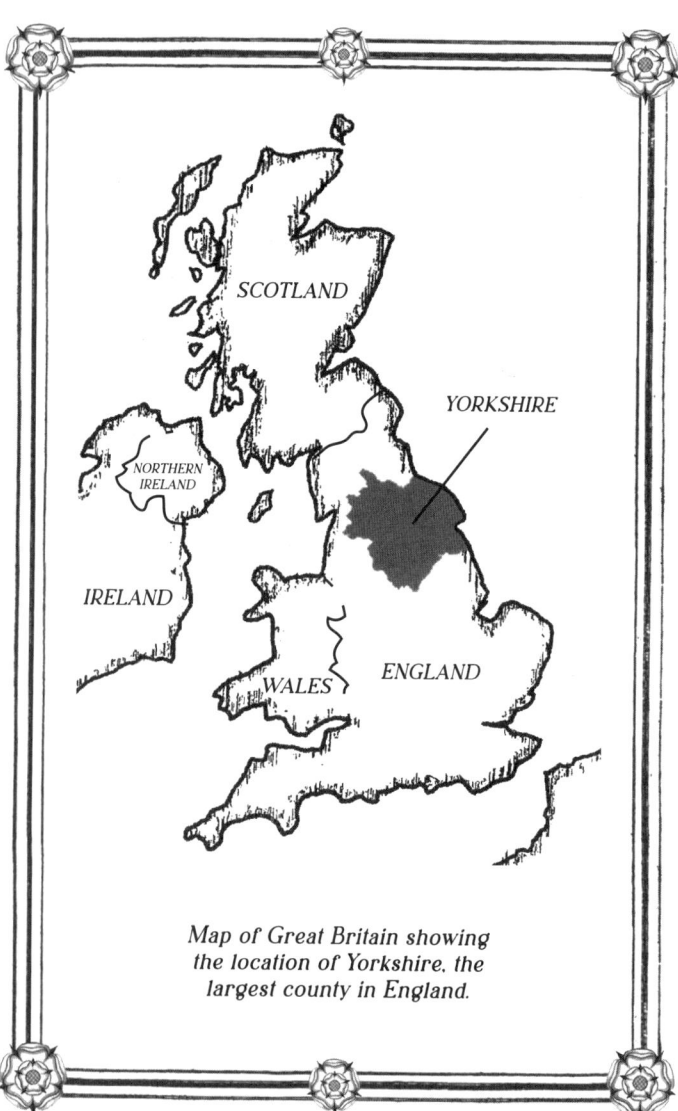

Map of Great Britain showing the location of Yorkshire, the largest county in England.

Introduction

Where the 'eck is Yorkshire?

Is it possible there are people in the world – or even in Britain – who do not know where Yorkshire is? Apparently there are, and if you happen to be one of them, you need to read the next few pages.

There was a time, not so very long ago, when British schools displayed huge roll-down maps of the British Isles on classroom walls, and school atlases had pages, usually at the front, devoted to British geography. This was how children learned about the nation's rivers, mountains, towns, transport networks and counties. Show them a map with the outlines of the counties, and they'd be able to name a good number of them, especially those close to where they lived.

It's different today, and children can sail through their school years without learning that the Severn is Britain's longest river (354 km / 220 miles), that Ben Nevis is the highest mountain (1,344 m / 4,409 ft), or that there are 86 historic or traditional counties.[1] Give today's youngsters an outline map of British counties to name, and many would be left blank, or misplaced (counties, that is, not children).

Could you do any better? Could you pick out, say, Derbyshire from Nottinghamshire, Brecknockshire from Radnorshire, or Morayshire from Banffshire? Could you be certain of pointing to Yorkshire and – heaven forbid – not its arch-rival Lancashire?

So, for the benefit of the geographically-challenged, here are a few basic facts to help you locate the fine county of Yorkshire on your mental map of the British Isles.

---

1. *39 in England, 34 in Scotland, 13 in Wales.*

Location, location, location

Yorkshire is in the north of England.[1]

*

To put it another way, Yorkshire is halfway up the map of Britain, on the right-hand side.

*

York, the county town, is closer to Edinburgh, capital of Scotland, than it is to London, capital of England. A straight line to Edinburgh is 259 km (161 miles), but the line to London is an extra 21 km (13 miles). It's not much, but it's more than enough to make the point that Yorkshirefolk are true northerners (and proud of it). The fact that London and the south are a long way from God's Own County, as they call it, suits them just fine.

*

Yorkshire almost splits Britain in two, reaching from the North Sea on the east coast to within touching distance of the Irish Sea on the west coast. The county's most westerly place, Low Bentham, is a mere 24 km (15 miles) from the sea, and it's only a lump of Lancashire that stops Yorkshire stretching from coast to coast.

---

1. There's no firm line to divide England's north from south. Some say the north begins at the Watford Gap - a break in the hills in the county of Northamptonshire. Others say it begins further up the country at Crewe, in Cheshire, a railway town hailed by travellers as the 'gateway to the north'.

Yorkshire A Very Peculiar History

Hopefully, this has fixed Yorkshire 'up north' in your mind, and you should have the idea that it's big. In fact, it's Britain's biggest county. From north to south Yorkshire is about 152 km (95 miles), and west to east 183 km (114 miles).

Yorkshire is so big that when the Vikings arrived in the AD 800s, they carved it up into three pieces that eventually became known as the Ridings of Yorkshire. The North, West and East Ridings served the county well for more than a thousand years. Civil wars and world wars came and went, and the Yorkshire Ridings survived

Ridings of Yorkshire

Why Ridings? Because the Viking word for the three pieces was 'thrithjungr', which became the Old English word 'thriding'. Try saying it – what does it sound like? Thriding became the modern English word 'riding'. It simply means 'thirds'.

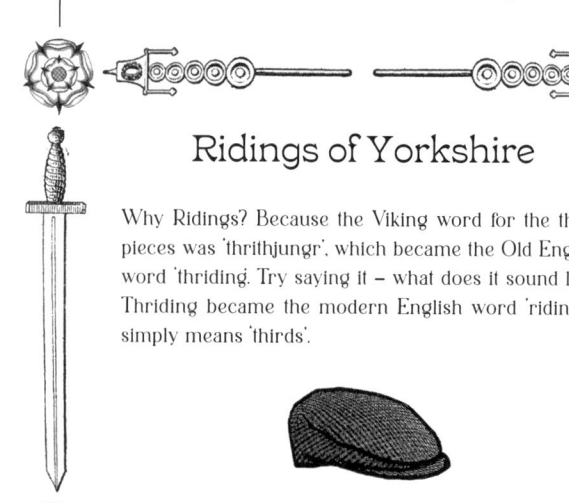

Where the 'eck is Yorkshire?

the lot until, on 1 April 1974, the government scrapped centuries of heritage across England and Wales.

It might have been April Fool's Day, but no one was laughing. When the Local Government Act of 1972 came into force in 1974, Yorkshirefolk woke up to a new-look county. Their ancient Ridings had gone, and were replaced by the new counties of North Yorkshire, West Yorkshire and South Yorkshire. Humberside was effectively East Yorkshire. But it was more than a change of a few old names. Civil servants had redrawn the county boundaries, and in a stroke of their pens did more to change the shape of Yorkshire than at any time since the Vikings.

So what is it like today? Well, for most Yorkshirefolk, Yorkshire means the historic county of Yorkshire – the county as it was before the government tinkered with it in 1974. It's that definition that this book will try to stick to, and as you turn the pages you'll be given an insight into the long, and sometimes peculiar, history of Yorkshire.

Chapter One

Prehistoric Yorkshire

Yorkshire's story begins a very long time ago. So long ago, you've got to go back to the end of the last Ice Age, which was about 10,000 years before the present day.

It's hard to say where Yorkshire's first people came from. There's a good chance they came from far away, perhaps from the mainland of Europe. If they did, they wouldn't have needed boats to make the long journey – they could have walked all the way. That was only possible because at the end of the last Ice Age the eastern side of Britain was joined to Europe by a land bridge – a big chunk of low-lying land

Yorkshire A Very Peculiar History

that archaeologists call Doggerland. It spread out from present-day East Anglia all the way down to Kent, then pushed east to join up with Holland, Germany and Denmark.

Today, the North Sea divides this area of Britain from Europe, but in the time we are talking about the sea level was lower. People and animals were able to wander back and forth between Britain and Europe across Doggerland.

Prehistoric Yorkshire

It may have been herds of migrating red deer and elk that led hunter-gatherers to cross Doggerland, tracking their prey northwards and up into Yorkshire. We know they came here because in 1947 archaeologists found a place where these early people set up camp.

Living by a lake

The ancient camp was discovered close to the villages of Flixton and Staxton, about 8 km (5 miles) south of Scarborough. Archaeologists have given it the name Star Carr[1], and their discoveries rewrote the history of early people not just in Yorkshire but in Britain.

It was around 8,700 BC that a group of hunter-gatherers arrived. Archaeologists call this period the Mesolithic, which means Middle Stone Age. The group came to the northern shore of a shallow lake, which spread across what is today the Vale of Pickering. Although the lake dried up long ago, its extent can be traced in the landscape of Yorkshire. It has even been given a name – Lake Pickering.

---

1. 'Carr' is a Yorkshire dialect word meaning 'marshy'.

Yorkshire A Very Peculiar History

The Star Carr camp was in use for about three hundred years. Throughout this time small bands of people came to the site, possibly each summer. They stayed a while, before moving on. From bones found at the site it's clear they hunted red deer and other wild animals, including hares and hedgehogs. Even though they were living at the edge of a lake, fish was off the menu as no fish bones were found by the archaeologists.

Fires were deliberately started along the shore of the lake, perhaps to burn away water reeds. It was a cunning trap. As new reeds grew, animals came to the edge of the lake to graze on the tasty shoots, and when they did, the hunters attacked them with spears and arrows.

Several masks were found at Star Carr, made from the front parts of red deer skulls with antlers still attached. Perhaps Yorkshire's Stone Age hunters wore the masks during hunts - either as disguises to help them creep close to their prey, or as magical items that they hoped would bring them good luck in the hunt.

Prehistoric Yorkshire

The people who came to the Star Carr camp – the most famous Mesolithic site in Britain – were not alone. Archaeologists returned to dig along the shores of the extinct Lake Pickering in the 1980s, and found more places where people had camped, some 10,000 years ago. They were back again in 2010, and this time found a 'house' – the oldest house ever found in Britain.

By around 6,500 BC, sea levels had risen and the low-lying Doggerland had been flooded. It had disappeared beneath the North Sea, making Britain an island for the first time, no longer joined to Europe by a land bridge.

"Stop lewkin' at me!"

It was a bad antler day for the hunter.

The Mesolithic was followed by the Neolithic, or New Stone Age, which began around 4,500 BC. It was a time of major changes, when people switched from a nomadic hunter-gatherer way of life and settled down to live in farming communities. The people of the Neolithic period were the first farmers.

Stonehenge of the North, in Yorkshire[1]

One of Britain's greatest Neolithic monuments is at Thornborough, near Ripon, North Yorkshire. There is little to be seen at ground level. To appreciate the monument it has to be seen from above, and only then do the banks and ditches of three huge circles come into view. These are the Thornborough Henges – earthworks from 3,500 BC, a thousand years older than the pyramids of Giza, Egypt. They have been dubbed the 'Stonehenge of the North' except, unlike the real Stonehenge 435 km (270 miles) to the south, there are no giant stones to be seen.

---

1. *Though Arbor Low in Staffordshire, 65 miles south, also makes this claim.*

Prehistoric Yorkshire

Each circle measures 240 m (790 ft) across, with earth banks that once stood at least 1.5 m (5 ft) high. When new, the banks were covered in gypsum crystals, making them stand out as three shining white rings, visible from a long way away. The henges are spaced evenly apart, separated from each other by a distance of about 500 m (1,650 ft).

Henges were one of the major structures of Neolithic Britain, and are found across much of the country. Usually circular, they are composed of an earth bank with a ditch on the inside (the soil dug out from the ditch was piled up to make the bank). One or two entrances were cut through the bank, allowing access to the space inside. Some, such as Stonehenge, had a circle of stones inside them, or around the outside.

The big question is: what were henges for? They have been called the 'cathedrals of their day', so perhaps they were sacred places were priests, elders and pilgrims came together to perform ceremonies and offer gifts to gods, spirits and ancestors. Is that what happened at Thornborough? You decide!

Bring on the Bronze Age

Around 2,000 BC the first metal tools and weapons appeared, made from copper and bronze. The Bronze Age had begun.

Yorkshire is rich in Bronze Age sites, especially burial mounds known as barrows. Many have names, such as Shunner Howe, Lilla Howe and Swarth Howe.[1] However, some of Yorkshire's best Bronze Age relics have been found not on dry land, but stuck in the mud of the River Humber, at North Ferriby, East Yorkshire. Three ancient wooden boats have been found here, and the Ferriby site has been described as the 'world's oldest boatyard'.

The people who paddled the Ferriby boats must have been some of the bravest sailors in history. They sailed along Britain's rivers, such as the Yorkshire Humber, and crossed the sea. Think of the boats as cargo vessels, lugging loads back and forth across the North Sea, shifting goods to and from Yorkshire.

---

1. 'Howe' is a Yorkshire dialect word meaning 'hill'.

Ferriby boat number 1

The first, and best preserved, of the Ferriby boats (Ferriby 1) was found in 1937.

*

It dates to about 1,200 BC, making it almost four thousand years old.

*

Enough of the ship survived to show that it had been more than 13 m (42 ft) long and 1.7 m (5 ft 6 in) wide.

*

It was made from thick planks of oak, joined together with lengths of twisted yew, which literally stitched one plank to the next, as if they were pieces of fabric.

*

To make the boat watertight, the gaps between the planks were stuffed with moss, and strips of oak were fixed over them.

*

It was a paddle boat, and would have been moved through the water by a team using wooden paddles.

Yorkshire A Very Peculiar History

Tribes and chariots

Around 700 BC metalworkers began using iron for tools and weapons. The Iron Age had begun. Now, for the first time in the history of Yorkshire, names can be given to the prehistoric people who lived there – and that's because the Romans wrote them down (thank you, Romans!).

Iron Age Britain was a tribal nation, and three tribes lived in Yorkshire. East Yorkshire was the homeland of the Parisii tribe, the Gabrantovices occupied North Yorkshire, but the tribe that controlled the most land, from the River Humber all the way up to Scotland, was the Brigantes.

The territory of the Brigantes, known as Brigantia, was the largest of all Britain's Iron Age tribes. The Brigantes had several major settlements in Yorkshire, some of which are mentioned by Roman writers. They included Catterick, Aldborough, Ilkley and York.

It's what's under the Yorkshire soil that makes the county's Iron Age unique in Britain. In East Yorkshire, at Wetwang Slack, Driffield, Arras,

Prehistoric Yorkshire

Eastburn and elsewhere, are hundreds of small burial barrows surrounded by square ditches. Why square and not round[1], no one knows, and they're only found in this one small area of Britain. Dug into the ground beneath the barrows are the graves of Yorkshire's Iron Age inhabitants.

Most were buried with a few grave goods – a clay pot, a joint of meat, bracelets, beads, a knife, sword and shield. But some were clearly the graves of important people, who were buried with two-wheeled vehicles. Usually referred to as 'chariots', they may have been carts or carriages – personal transport to carry the dead person to the next world.

Life (and death) for Iron Age people in Yorkshire probably seemed pretty good. There might have been the odd falling-out with a nearby tribe, and every so often a poor harvest would come along – but it wasn't the end of the world.

The end actually came from far away and over the sea, and the days of the Brigantes, and all the other Iron Age tribes, were numbered.

1. Most Iron Age burial mounds are round

Ten Things You Didn't Know About Prehistoric Yorkshire

1. The oldest signs of human activity in Yorkshire come from Victoria Cave, about 3 km (2 miles) north of Settle. A harpoon point made from deer antler was found here, dated to about 11,000 years ago.

2. Skeletons of two dogs were found at the Star Carr hunter-gatherer site, near Scarborough. At around 10,000 years old, they are among the oldest dogs found in Europe.

3. Britain's tallest standing stone is in Rudston, East Yorkshire. Known as the Rudston Monolith, it is 1.8m (6 ft) wide and 7.9m (26 ft) tall, and dates from about 1,600 BC.

4. The three henges at Thornborough line up with the three central stars in the belt of Orion, which appears in the night sky. Was this planned, or just a coincidence?

5. In 2003, a fire destroyed part of Fylingdales Moor, North Yorkshire. With the heather gone, archaeologists were able to spot hundreds of examples of Neolithic and Bronze Age rock art (stones decorated with patterns).

6. Superstitious people used to think Yorkshire's round barrows were the homes of irritating hobgoblins.

7. The Devil's Arrows are three Bronze Age standing stones at Boroughbridge, North Yorkshire. A local legend says the Devil threw them at the town of Aldborough, but they fell short and landed at Boroughbridge.

8. The Scamridge Dykes, a huge series of earthworks cutting across the countryside near Scalby, North Yorkshire, may be a Bronze Age or Iron Age boundary separating rival tribes.

9. The Iron Age hillfort[1] at Ingleborough, West Yorkshire, is one of the highest in Britain, 716 m (2,350 ft) above sea level.

10. An Iron Age log boat almost 13 m (42 ft) long was found at Hasholme, East Yorkshire, in 1984. It was made from a hollowed-out oak tree in about 300 BC, and sank carrying a cargo of beef and timber.

A monolith standing stone

---

1. Hillforts were sited on the tops of hills, and were surrounded by deep ditches and tall banks. Inside were houses and storage places for food, and it's thought they provided safe havens for local communities in times of trouble.

VENERUNT, VIDERUNT, VICERUNT... REGRESSI SUNT AD DOMUM.

(THEY CAME, THEY SAW, THEY CONQUERED... THEN THEY WENT HOME.)

Chapter Two

Roman Yorkshire

The year AD 43 was a good one for the Romans, but not for the native peoples of Britain. That was the year an invasion force of some 40,000 Roman soldiers crossed the Oceanus Britannicus (the British Sea, which we call the English Channel). They set about making Britain a province of the Roman Empire.

The Roman army landed in east Kent, possibly at Richborough, which became the gateway to Britain. From there they headed to Camulodunum (modern Colchester), the capital of the Trinovantes tribe. The fall of Camulodunum in the summer of AD 43 was the start of the Roman conquest of Britain. Some tribes fought the Romans. However, others were friendly. Among the friendly tribes was the Brigantes – the tribe whose territory covered much of northern England, including Yorkshire. The Romans claimed eleven British rulers had surrendered to them at Camulodunum, and it's thought that Queen Cartimandua, ruler of the Brigantes, was one.

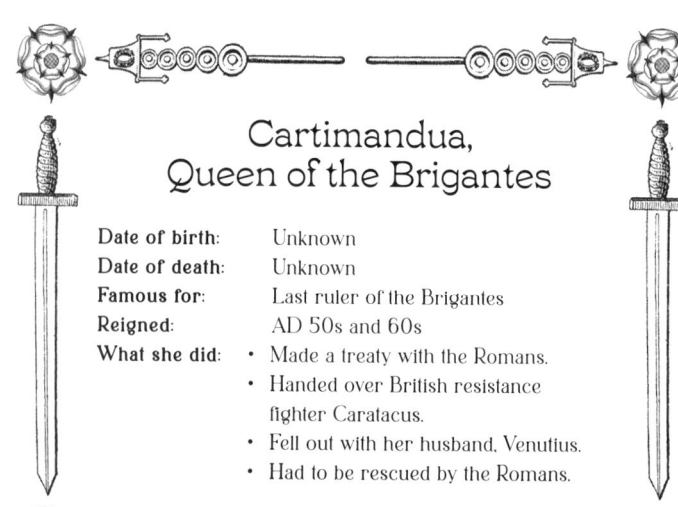

Cartimandua, Queen of the Brigantes

Date of birth: Unknown
Date of death: Unknown
Famous for: Last ruler of the Brigantes
Reigned: AD 50s and 60s
What she did:
- Made a treaty with the Romans.
- Handed over British resistance fighter Caratacus.
- Fell out with her husband, Venutius.
- Had to be rescued by the Romans.

Roman Yorkshire

Cartimandua showed her support for the Romans in AD 51, when she gave them Caratacus. He was a British leader who had fought the Romans, and had fled north to the kingdom of the Brigantes where he hoped Cartimandua would shelter him. Big mistake for Caratacus and for Cartimandua.

Caratacus wasn't the only Briton to feel betrayed by Cartimandua. Her husband, King Venutius, fell out with her, and the couple were divorced. It was only a matter of time before civil war broke out among the Brigantes – Venutius versus Cartimandua.

Things came to a head in AD 68 or 69, when Venutius tried to overthrow Cartimandua. This was a headache for the Romans. The last thing they wanted was for Venutius to start a rebellion of the British tribes.

The Romans sent a task force of cavalry and foot soldiers into Brigantian territory. They rescued Cartimandua, leaving Venutius in control of the Brigantes. The tribe was now hostile to the Romans – their one-time friend had become the enemy of Rome.

Yorkshire A Very Peculiar History

The Romans conquer Yorkshire

In AD 71 a new governor was put in charge of Britain. He was Quintus Petillius Cerialis, and he decided to sort out the Brigantes. The way to do this was to conquer them. Unfortunately, not a lot is known about the military campaign of Cerialis in Yorkshire. However, a Roman writer called Tacitus said this about it:

"Cerialis at once struck terror into their hearts by attacking the state of the Brigantes, which is said to be the most populous tribe in the whole province. After a series of battles - some of them bloody - Cerialis had conquered the major part of their territory."

It's known that Cerialis headed north into Brigantia from his base at Lindum (modern Lincoln) with the 6,000 men of the Ninth Legion (IX Hispana). Once inside enemy territory, he set up a temporary military camp at a place where two rivers met, the Ouse and its tributary, the Foss. The camp grew into a fort known to the Romans as Eboracum, which, in time,

Roman Yorkshire

became the city of York. To conquer the unruly Brigantes, the Roman battle plan was to attack the tribe's capital at Stanwick, North Yorkshire.

As the Roman force approached Stanwick, Venutius was forced out in an attempt to halt the attack. Britons and Romans clashed somewhere in the vicinity of Scotch Corner, a short distance south of the Brigantian capital. It was the last stand of Venutius. The British king was defeated, and he fled to the western edge of Brigantian territory in Lancashire and Cumbria. The Romans took control of most of Brigantia,

"Clear off, you wretched Brits!"

and to make sure it stayed that way, Governor Cerialis stationed the Ninth Legion at the fort of Eboracum. Roads were built, such as Icknield Street, which brought traffic from the south, and Dere Street, which took travellers north from Eboracum.

More forts were built across Brigantia, and the ones at Piercebridge, just outside North Yorkshire, and at Ilkley, West Yorkshire, were positioned to protect routes from the north and the west - routes which the native Britons might have used to attack the Romans.

By around AD 80 the threat from the Brigantes was over. They had been pacified, and the Roman conquest of their territory - Yorkshire and beyond - was complete.

"Who wants to play Brit in the middle?"

Roman Yorkshire

York under the Romans

The first Roman fort at Eboracum was a cluster of wooden barracks, officers' quarters and stores surrounded by an earth rampart (wall). Along the top of the rampart was a timber palisade (fence), and there were also timber watchtowers.

By the AD 100s the buildings and rampart had been rebuilt in stone. The fort had become a fortress, and for the next three hundred years Eboracum was the headquarters of the Roman army in northern Britain.

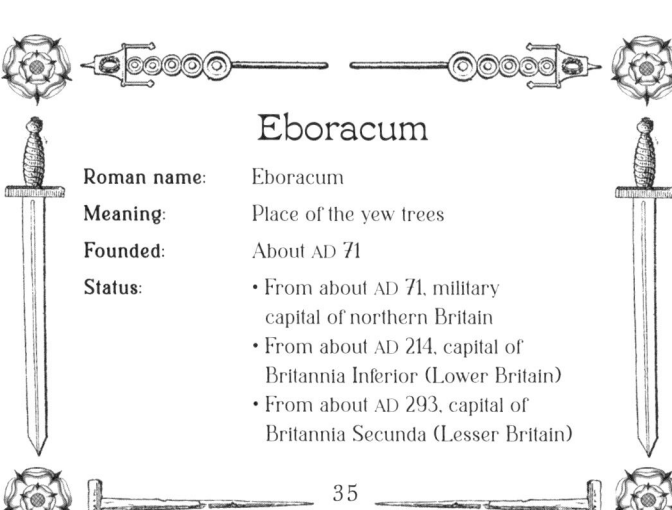

Eboracum

Roman name: Eboracum

Meaning: Place of the yew trees

Founded: About AD 71

Status:
- From about AD 71, military capital of northern Britain
- From about AD 214, capital of Britannia Inferior (Lower Britain)
- From about AD 293, capital of Britannia Secunda (Lesser Britain)

It didn't take long for civilians to come to Eboracum, and a thriving settlement grew up outside the fortress and on the opposite bank of the River Ouse. In the AD 200s the settlement became a *colonia* (colony) – an honour bestowed on only three other Roman towns in Britain.[1] It was a way of marking Eboracum out as a Roman town in every sense – the best sort of town in the Roman world, where Roman citizens lived and where Roman soldiers settled after they had left the army.

Eboracum was a far-flung outpost of the Roman Empire, about as far away from the city of Rome as it was possible to be (about 1,675 km / 1,042 miles). Despite the great distance from the capital of the Roman Empire, Eboracum played an important part in Roman history, and several Roman emperors were linked with it. In fact, two emperors actually died in Eboracum.

---

1. *Camulodunum (Colchester), Lindum (Lincoln) and Glevum (Gloucester).*

Roman emperors connected with York

Hadrian	Visited York, AD 122
Severus	Died in York, AD 211
Constantius I	Died in York, AD 306
Constantine	Son of Constantius, proclaimed emperor in York, AD 306

The end of Roman Yorkshire

Eboracum fell into decline in the AD 300s. The population shrank, buildings were abandoned and roads were not looked after. The same was happening in towns across Roman Britain. Then, in the early AD 400s, the Roman legions in Britain were withdrawn in order to protect other parts of the Roman Empire. A new chapter in the history of Yorkshire was about to begin.

Ten Things You Didn't Know About Roman Yorkshire

1. There's a Roman sewer under York, at the corner of Church Street and Swinegate. It's 1 m (3 ft) high and 45 cm (18 in) wide, and has been traced for 52 m (170 ft). It carried water away from a Roman bathhouse.

2. A grain store in Coney Street, York, became infested with beetles. The Romans knocked it down, covered it with clay to seal in the bugs, then built a new store on top.

3. When York railway station was built in 1875, workmen cleared a Roman cemetery out of the way. Inside a stone coffin they found the skeleton of a girl. Her hair had not rotted away. You can see the girl's hair in the Yorkshire Museum, just as it was 1,700 years ago, still tied in bun.

4. In 1941 a large floor mosaic was found at a Roman villa at Brantingham, near Brough, East Yorkshire. In 1948, the mosaic was stolen. It has never been recovered. A second mosaic from the villa is in Hull Museum.

5. In 2007, David and Andrew Whelan (father and son) used metal detectors to search a field near the Roman town of Aldborough, North Yorkshire. They uncovered a treasure trove of medieval objects, including 617 silver coins, a gold arm ring and a gilt silver vessel. The hoard dated back to the early 10th Century.

6. Stonegate and Petergate are two main streets in York, which cross at right angles. They began as roads through the Roman fortress of Eboracum. Petergate was the Via Principalis, and Stonegate was the Via Praetoria. Another street, Chapter House Lane, was the Via Decumana.

7. York Minster, York's great medieval cathedral, was built on top of the Roman military headquarters building (the principia). Parts of the Roman building can be seen in the Minster's undercroft, 4.5 m (15 ft) below the present-day ground level.

8. Roman York was a multicultural town. For example, the skeleton of a woman from North Africa has been found. She is known as the Ivory Bangle Lady, because she was buried with an elephant ivory bangle.

9. In the AD 100s, the Romans established a pottery industry at Cantley, near Doncaster, South Yorkshire. The potters who worked there made cooking pots. Some of the potters' names are known, such as Sarrius, who worked there in about AD 170.

10. A cemetery found in the back gardens of Driffield Terrace, York, may be a gladiators' graveyard. Many of the skeletons were headless, as if they had been executed. One had bite marks from a lion, tiger or bear. The man might have died fighting wild animals in an arena.

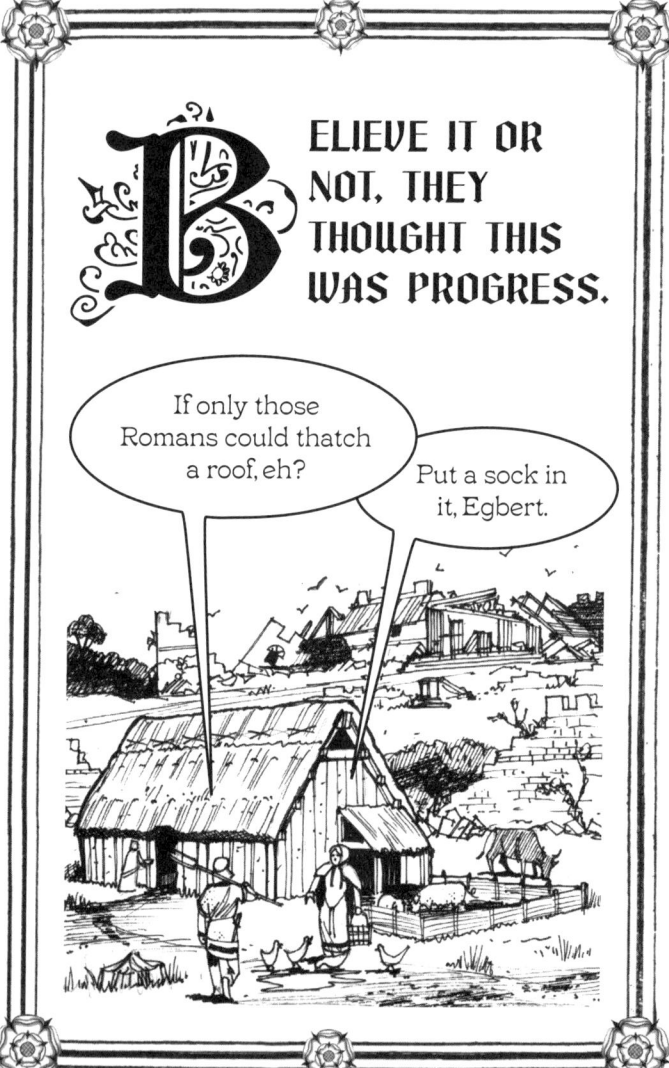

Chapter Three

Between the Romans and the Vikings

A new period in Yorkshire's history began in the early AD 400s. It spanned about four hundred years, from the departure of the Romans to the arrival of the Vikings in the AD 800s. This period used to be called the Dark Ages. It was a way of saying that after the Romans left, Britain became an uncivilised, unsafe place, as if society had broken down and had taken a step backwards to a darker, dangerous time.

Today's archaeologists and historians don't like calling this period the 'Dark Ages'. They say it was not 'dark' at all, but a time when the future of Britain was shaped. They prefer to call the bit between the Romans and the Vikings the 'Early Middle Ages'. It's not such a catchy label, but it is a fairer one to use.

The kingdom of Deira

After the Romans left, a struggle began for control of Britain. The country was split into kingdoms. It's thought that most of Yorkshire fell under control of the kingdom of Ebrauc, a name that came from Eboracum, the Roman name for York. However, Ebrauc was soon replaced by the kingdom of Deira, which was founded by settlers called Angles (it's not clear where the name Deira comes from).

The Angles came from what is now Denmark and north Germany, and while they were settling in Yorkshire, other Germanic peoples (Saxons and Jutes) were forming rival kingdoms to the south. Together, these are known as Anglo-Saxon kingdoms, from which the country of England[1] was eventually created.

At first, the Anglian kingdom of Deira relatively small. It first started in East Yorkshire in the

---

1. *The Angles gave their name to England, which means 'land of the Angles'.*

— Between the Romans and the Vikings —

AD 450s (or even before), but by the early AD 600s Deira covered the whole of Yorkshire. York was the capital of Deira, and the Angles called it Eoforwic, meaning 'wild-boar town'.

Archaeologists know when they have dug down to Eoforwic, as they come across a deep layer of what they call 'dark earth'. It's a soil layer that lies on top of the Roman levels – a clear sign that the buildings and roads of Roman York were not cared for after the Romans left. Only the headquarters of the old Roman fortress was kept in use by the Anglian settlers.

The Angles were not used to living in towns as the Romans had done. Instead, they were used to living in villages, one of which has been found at West Heslerton, North Yorkshire. Excavations there have uncovered the outlines of about two hundred wooden buildings, making it one of the largest digs of an Anglo-Saxon village anywhere in England. The village, which was spread out over a wide area, had houses, workshops and stores. It was occupied for about five hundred years, until it was deserted around AD 850. Villages like this were dotted across the Yorkshire landscape.

Yorkshire A Very Peculiar History

The kingdom of Northumbria

The Angles were incomers to Yorkshire. The locals were the native Britons, who weren't too

Places

1. Eoforwic
2. West Heslerton
3. Lindisfarne

Battle sites

4. Catterick
5. Hatfield Chase
6. Winwidfield

Between the Romans and the Vikings

keen on sharing their land with the settlers, invaders, outsiders – call them what you will.

Battles were fought across Britain between native British and Germanic peoples. In Yorkshire, the Battle of Catterick was fought in about AD 600, between Britons and Angles. It was a victory for the Angles.

A few years later, the Anglian kingdom of Deira joined with the neighbouring Anglian kingdom of Bernicia to form Northumbria – a vast Anglo-Saxon kingdom which covered much of northern England and southern Scotland. Eoforwic, the capital of Deira, now became the capital of Northumbria. On Easter Day, AD 627, King Edwin of Northumbria was baptised at Eoforwic by Paulinus, the first Bishop of York. This was a big step for Edwin to take. His baptism was a sign of his conversion from paganism to Christianity. What was good enought for the king was also good enough for the people of Northumbria, and many followed his example.

The rise of Eoforwic

King Edwin was baptised in a wooden church built on his orders.[1] It's possible that he had a royal palace at Eoforwic, but no trace of one has ever been found. There were probably old Roman buildings still standing, and it's thought he might have converted those to his royal residence. One thing is clear, though, the walls of the old Roman fortress were patched up and strengthened, and a stone tower was added. Known as the Anglian Tower, it is the only one of its kind in Britain, and it may date from the AD 600s.

Strengthening the walls was a sign of the times, as the 600s was a period of unrest between the rival Anglo-Saxon kingdoms. For Northumbria, the biggest threat came from the kingdom of Mercia, based in what is today the English Midlands.

---

1. *The wooden church was later enlarged and rebuilt in stone, and eventually it grew into the world-famous York Minster, one of the finest medieval cathedrals in Europe.*

Between the Romans and the Vikings

In AD 633, King Edwin's Northumbrian army clashed with a combined Mercian and Welsh army in the Battle of Hatfield Chase, near Doncaster, South Yorkshire. The Northumbrians lost, and Edwin was killed.

The Northumbrians had to wait until AD 655 for their revenge, and in the Battle of Winwaed, which may have been near Leeds, West Yorkshire, they defeated the Mercians and killed Penda, the Mercian king.

For the next one hundred years, Northumbria and Mercia remained enemies. They could have carried on squabbling with each other, but in AD 793, the Anglo-Saxon kingdoms of England faced a new danger.

That was the year raiders from Scandinavia attacked a monastery on Lindisfarne, an island off the coast of Northumbria. It was a signal the Vikings were coming, and the Anglo-Saxon town of Eoforwic, which used to be the Roman town of Eboracum, was about to face the fury of the Northmen – and get another new name.

Chapter Four

Viking Yorkshire

Next it was the turn of the Vikings to pick on little Britain. The Anglo-Saxon kingdom of Northumbria, of which Yorkshire was at the southern end, felt the full force of the land-grabbing, slave-taking, money-pinching Vikings. A book, the *Anglo-Saxon Chronicle*, recorded the very first Viking raid. It said:

"AD 793: *In this year terrible portents appeared over Northumbria, which sorely frightened the inhabitants: there were exceptional flashes of lightning, and fiery dragons were seen flying through the air. A great famine followed hard upon these signs; and a little later in that same year, on the 8th June, the harrying of the heathen miserably destroyed God's church in Lindisfarne."*

These were frightening times indeed. Alcuin of York (c.737–804), the town's most famous Anglo-Saxon scholar, described the fear that everyone was feeling. He said: *"Never before has such a terror appeared in Britain as we have now suffered from a pagan race, nor was it thought an inroad from the sea could be made."*

Look at Alcuin's words again: *"...nor was it thought an inroad from the sea could be made."* He's saying that everyone thought Britain was safe because it was an island surrounded by sea – a barrier to protect Britain. Wrong! The Vikings were the supreme boat-builders and sailors of the time, and Britain was just a few days' sail away from their homelands in what is Norway and Denmark. To them, the North Sea was the 'main road' that led straight to new land, new riches and new lives.

Viking Yorkshire

An army on the move

For the next fifty years, the Vikings were little more than seasonal pests. Each summer they crossed the North Sea and raided a few places, carrying loot and slaves back to Scandinavia.

Then, in AD 865, a large force of Vikings landed in East Anglia – and this time they were here to stay. The Anglo-Saxons called it the Great Heathen Army, or the Great Army. The Vikings were on a mission – to capture as much land in Britain as possible.

From East Anglia, they headed north and in AD 866 crossed the River Humber into Yorkshire. The *Anglo-Saxon Chronicle* describes what happened:

"In this year the heathen army went from East Anglia over the mouth of the Humber to York in Northumbria ... and there was immense slaughter of the Northumbrians, some within York, and some without, and the survivors made peace with the heathen army."

Yorkshire A Very Peculiar History

In other words, the Vikings fought the locals and won, and they captured York. It was the first important English town captured by the invaders. Until then, York had been known by its Anglo-Saxon name of Eoforwic, but when the Vikings moved in they gave it a new name – Jorvik (say: yor-vik).

Jorvik under the Vikings

For the first few years after its capture, the Vikings hardly bothered with York. Most of the Great Army was busy in the south of England, trying to defeat the Anglo-Saxon kingdom of Wessex.[1] But, when an uprising against the Vikings started in the north in AD 872, the Great Army headed back to sort the locals out – which they did.

After this, some of the Vikings settled in and around Jorvik, and a Viking leader called Halfdan handed out land to his warriors. He became the first of a long line of Viking kings to rule Jorvik, the capital of the Viking kingdom in England.

---

1. This they never did, as Alfred the Great, king of Wessex, defeated them in battle in AD 878. Peace was agreed (the Treaty of Wedmore) and England was divided between the English and the Vikings. The Vikings were allowed to live in northern and eastern England, in an area known as the Danelaw. The English held the south and west.

Viking Yorkshire

Jorvik grew into a thriving Viking town, complete with the customs and crafts of Scandinavia. New streets were built, many of which are still part of today's town plan. Even the narrow-fronted plots on which York's shops stand were laid out by the Viking's.

Some of York's Viking streets end in *-gate*, which comes from the Old Norse[1] word *gata* meaning 'street' (Jubbergate, Micklegate and Hungate are examples). York's best-known Viking street is Coppergate, which means 'street of the woodworkers'. It's nothing to do with copper! Rather, it comes from the word Cooper.

In the 1970s and 1980s, Viking buildings were found in Coppergate, dating from the AD 900s. Made from planks of timber, they were so well preserved that even after a thousand years parts of them were still almost 2 m (6 ft) high. From the amount of wood shavings found, it was clear they were the workshops and homes of Viking woodworkers.

1. The language of the Vikings.

Yorkshire A Very Peculiar History

Kings of Jorvik

King	Dates of reign
Halfdan	871-77
Guthfrith	c.883-95
Sigfrid	c.895-900
Cnut	c.900-2
Aethelwald*	903
Halfdan II	902-910
Eowils	902-910
Ivar	902-910
Ragnald	c.911, 919-21
Sihtric Caech	921-7
Guthfrith II	927
Athelstan*	927-39
Olaf Guthfrithsson	939-41
Olaf Sihtricsson	941-4
Ragnald Guthfrithson	943-4
Edmund I*	944-6
Eadred*	946-8
Erik Bloodaxe	948
Olaf Sihtricsson	949-52
Erik Bloodaxe	952-4

* English kings who ruled Jorvik in between the Viking ones.

Viking Yorkshire

It wasn't only wooden objects that were made in the workshops of Coppergate. Amber was shaped into beads, antler and bone were cut to make combs, and somewhere nearby a moneyer hammered out silver pennies in the town's mint (a place where coins were made). Two of his iron dies – the tools that stamped the design on to the pennies – turned up in the Coppergate dig.[1]

Cutaway view of a Viking workshop

1. One of the dies was for making pennies in about AD 920, but as none have been matched to it (thousands have been checked), it may never have been used.

Yorkshire A Very Peculiar History

Drink like a Viking

Apple pips have been found in Jorvik, so perhaps the town's Viking population enjoyed this sweet apple drink.

Ingredients:

- 2 pints (950 ml) water
- 4 apples
- honey

Method:

- Chop the apples into small pieces (don't peel them, and don't cut out the cores).
- Add the water and chopped apples to a pan, then simmer for a few minutes.
- Add a dollop of honey and stir in.
- Take off the heat and leave to cool.
- Pour into cups, bits and all, then sip.

The end of Viking Yorkshire

The Vikings came to Yorkshire as warriors, and ended up staying. For about eighty years all seemed well. However, plans were being hatched by the English, who wanted to unite England into one nation. That meant taking the kingdom of Northumbria, of which Yorkshire was a part, back from the Vikings.

It was Athelstan (c.895–939), king of Wessex, who got down to the serious business of nation-making. He seized Jorvik in AD 927, then defeated an army of Vikings, Scots and Britons at the Battle of Brunanburgh (AD 937). Some say it was fought in Yorkshire on the banks of the River Don, between Rotherham and Sheffield. Athelstan's victory was a milestone in the unification of England – but the job was far from finished as the Northumbrians had a plan of their own.

After many years of living together, the Vikings had become part of Northumbrian society. For many Northumbrians, the last thing they wanted was to be ruled by the upstart English from the south – so they invited Eric Haraldsson, king of Norway, to become king of Jorvik. Because of his violent nature, he is better known by his nickname – Eric Bloodaxe. His reign was short, and in AD 954, at the Battle of Stainmore, on the western edge of North Yorkshire, he was killed by an English army. With the death of Eric Bloodaxe, Viking rule at Jorvik was over, and Northumbria – which included Yorkshire – was absorbed into the emerging kingdom of England. For the next one hundred years, Yorkshire was at peace – that is until 1066, when the county once again found itself centre stage of English history.

Signposts to the past

You can tell the Vikings were in Yorkshire from clues in the names of towns and villages. Lots of Yorkshire places have Old Norse in them.

Ends in	Means	Place
-by	farm, town	Wetherby
-thwaite	village	Yockenthwaite
-thorpe	clearing	Scagglethorpe
-toft	homestead	Langtoft

Five Things You Didn't Know About Viking Yorkshire

1. The Lloyds Bank coprolite is a fossilised Viking poo dug up in York, beneath the site of what was to become a branch of a bank. It is more colloquially known as the Lloyds Bank turd. It is said to be the biggest preserved human poo ever found (23 cm / 9 in long). In 2003, the rock-hard poo was dropped, and broke into three bits.

2. In 2007, David and Andrew Whelan (the same pair who found a Roman lead coffin: see page 38), unearthed the Vale of York Viking Hoard – a bowl with 617 silver coins and other valuables. This treasure is now in the Yorkshire Museum, York.

3. The Cawood Sword, one of the best Viking swords ever found, was pulled from the River Ouse at Cawood, North Yorkshire, in the 1800s.

4. In total, an incredible 40,000 objects were uncovered in the dig at Coppergate. Some 36,000 layers of soil were excavated, and 8 tons of soil were sieved!

5. There are 210 '-by' and 155 '-thorpe' place names in use in Yorkshire today. Nowhere else in Britain has this many places with Scandinavian connections.

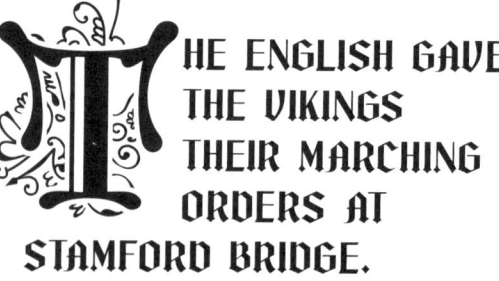

THE ENGLISH GAVE THE VIKINGS THEIR MARCHING ORDERS AT STAMFORD BRIDGE.

Chapter Five

Norman Yorkshire

By the year 1000, York had a population of about 8,000, and was the second largest town in England after London. It was also a 'shire town' – the leading town in its shire[1] or area. York gave its name to its shire, and that's how Yorkshire became Yorkshire. It was one of many shires formed during the AD 900s, following the unification of England, when the Anglo-Saxon kingdoms of Northumbria, Mercia and Wessex had come together, under the rule of one king.

---

1. From the Old English 'scir'. When the Normans arrived, it was replaced with their French word 'conté', from which comes the English word 'county'.

Yorkshire A Very Peculiar History

The first known use in writing of the name 'Yorkshire' dates from 1065, when it appeared in the *Anglo-Saxon Chronicle*. However, it would have been called Yorkshire in everyday speech before this date.

As a new (or at least newish) English shire, Yorkshire must have seemed set for great things. York was a thriving and prosperous town, and was home to one of England's busiest ports. But then, in 1066, the good times came to a sudden and dramatic end – not just for Yorkshire, but for all England.

In the year 1066...

- One king died peacefully
- Two kings were killed in battle
- Two foreign armies invaded England
- Three battles were fought
- Three kings wore the crown of England

Norman Yorkshire

Rivals for the crown

Trouble began on 5 January 1066, when King Edward[1] (reigned 1042–66) died. The question then was: *Who should be the next king?* It was a hard question to answer because:

- Edward had no children, so there was no one to inherit the crown.

- Prince Edgar, a relative, was ruled out because he was only a 14-year-old boy.

- The crown would have to pass to whoever had the strongest claim to it.

Three men thought they had the best claim to become the next king of England:

1. **Harold Sigurdsson**. He was the King of Norway, and was nicknamed 'Harold Hardrada', meaning 'Harold the Stern'. He believed the crown of England had been promised to his family. Under Harold Hardrada, England would be ruled by a Norwegian king.

---

1. Known as Edward the Confessor because he spent much time praying and confessing his sins to God.

Yorkshire A Very Peculiar History

2. **William, Duke of Normandy.**[1] In 1051, King Edward had promised the English throne to Duke William, his second cousin. Under William, England would be ruled by a Norman king.

3. **Harold Godwinson.** He was the Earl of Wessex and was from a leading Saxon family. Harold was King Edward's brother-in-law and was the most powerful man in England after the king. As King Edward lay dying, he named Harold as his successor. By doing this, Edward broke his promise to Duke William. Under Harold, England would be ruled by an English king.

The day after Edward's death, Harold Godwinson was crowned King Harold II by Ealdred, the Archbishop of York. Not surprisingly, Duke William, who thought he would be king, felt betrayed. He decided to invade England and take the crown from Harold. As bad luck would have it, Harold Hardrada of Norway had the same idea.

---

1. Normandy is a region in the north of France.

Norman Yorkshire

Yorkshire at War

In September 1066, Hardrada sailed from Norway with an army. On 20 September, at Fulford Gate, near York, the invaders were met by an English army, and the first of the year's three battles was fought. The English lost, and Hardrada captured York.

Five days later came the year's second battle, at Stamford Bridge, also near York. This time it was a victory for the English, led by King Harold Godwinson, who had marched an army from London. Hardrada was killed – the first of the kings to die in battle that year.

Here come the Normans!

With King Harold busy in Yorkshire, Duke William seized his opportunity to invade England. His army of about 7,500 Normans crossed the English Channel and landed at Pevensey, Sussex, on 28 September. The Norman invasion was underway.

Yorkshire A Very Peculiar History

King Harold led his English army back from Yorkshire, and on 14 October 1066, the third and bloodiest battle of the year was fought - the Battle of Hastings.[1] At one point a rumour spread that Duke William had been killed, and it looked as if the English would triumph. But then, in the afternoon, according to the Bayeaux Tapestry, King Harold was shot in the eye by an arrow, then possibly hacked to death by Norman soldiers - the second king to die in battle that fateful year.

A battle between Normans and Saxons, taken from the Bayeux Tapestry

In London, on Christmas Day, 1066, Ealdred, Archbishop of York, crowned Duke William, making him King William I (reigned 1066-87).

---

1. *The battle was fought along a ridge, about 11 km (7 miles) from Hastings, Sussex. The English called the ridge Santlache ('Sandy Stream'), but years later it was given the Norman name 'Senlac' (French for 'Blood Lake').*

The way was clear for the Norman Conquest of England, and William would go down in history as 'William the Conqueror'.

The Harrying of the North

Northern England felt the full force of the Normans, as William's army moved fast to crush a rebellion in Yorkshire. The Normans reached York in 1068, and the town was quickly taken. William ordered a castle to be built, followed by a second in 1069. Both were attacked, after which the Normans went on a campaign of ruthless violence - the 'Harrying[1] of the North'.

Nothing and no one was spared. In the winter of 1069-70, Norman troops destroyed villages, crops and livestock not only in Yorkshire but also in the Midlands.

The loss of life and land was especially violent in Yorkshire, where some 480 villages were laid to waste and another 314 were ravaged. Orderic Vitalis (1075-c.1142), an English monk,

---

1. The verb 'harry' means to ravage or destroy.

described the harrying in Yorkshire: "*Nowhere else had William shown so much cruelty.*" Another monk, Symeon of Durham (c.1090-c.1128), said: "*It was horrible to observe, in houses, streets and roads, human corpses rotting. No one survived to cover them with earth.*"

The Normans got what they wanted - peace, but at a terrible price. Orderic claimed 100,000 people had died, either at the end of Norman swords or from starvation (though he might have exaggerated the death toll). The Normans emerged as lords and masters of the English, whose land they seized then handed out to Norman aristocrats as rewards.

After the harrying, Yorkshire was a broken county. The surviving population was subdued, villages were deserted and areas of land were barren. Even York, the county town, was not spared, with half its houses destroyed or derelict. It was a low point in Yorkshire's history, but as the Norman grip tightened, a period of recovery and rebuilding began.

Domesday Book, Yorkshire

In 1086, the Domesday Book was compiled – a detailed survey of the counties of England. It provides a snapshot of Norman England, giving details about the size of towns and villages, who owned what, and how much it was worth. Here's what it recorded for the Ridings of Yorkshire:

	Places	Population
East Riding	424	2,363
West Riding	719	3,192
North Riding	639	2,014
Totals	**1,782**	**7,569**[1]

1. *As only the heads of families were counted, experts think this number must be multiplied by four or five to give some idea of Yorkshire's 11th-century population, putting it at anything from 30,000 to 40,000.*

Ten Things You Didn't Know About Norman Yorkshire

1. The Normans created forests, where the Norman elite hunted wild boar and deer. The Forest of Knaresborough, North Yorkshire, was the largest at 32 km (20 miles) long and 13 km (8 miles) wide.

2. William de Warenne, one of King William's most trusted men, was given a lot of land, including King Harold's royal estate at Conisbrough, South Yorkshire. By 1086, twenty years after the Battle of Hastings, Warenne was the fourth-richest man in England, with estates in twelve counties.

3. Richmond, North Yorkshire, owes its name to the Normans. They called it Riche Mont, meaning 'strong hill'. The French name eventually became Richmond.

4. The village of Bolton Percy, North Yorkshire, takes its name from its first Norman lord, William de Percy, who came from Percy-en-Auge, Normandy.

5. Between 2008 and 2009, 178 Norman silver pennies from the reign of Henry I (a son of William the Conqueror) were found in a field at Knaresborough, North Yorkshire.

6. A Norman toilet seat was found by archaeologists during excavations at Coppergate, York. It was a plank of wood with a bottom-sized hole in it, worn smooth by years of sitters.

7. Norman Yorkshire has been described as a 'border zone' between Scotland and England. In 1138, a Scottish army invaded the county, and was defeated at Northallerton, North Yorkshire, in the Battle of the Standard.

8. The coast of East Yorkshire, particularly Holderness, is eroded by the sea and over the centuries more than twenty villages have been washed away, such as Sand le Mere, which had ceased to exist by 1086, when the Domesday Book was compiled.

9. The first, known reference to a windmill in England is from 1185. The mill was at Weedley, near South Cave, East Yorkshire. The windmill is long gone – and so is the village.

10. Towards the end of his life, William the Conqueror seemed to regret the Norman violence in Yorkshire. He is reputed to have said:

    "I have persecuted its native inhabitants beyond all reason ... innumerable multitudes, especially in the county of York, perished through me by famine or the sword."

Chapter Six

Castles and Cathedrals

The castles and cathedrals of Yorkshire are among the best known in the country, from the windswept Scarborough Castle to the soaring towers of York Minster. These, and many others, are tourist magnets today, each with a story to tell about turbulent times, powerful families and faithful pilgrims.

Yorkshire A Very Peculiar History

Castles made of earth

It was the Normans who brought castle-building to Yorkshire, and the one built at York in 1068 was among the first Norman castles built on English soil.[1] In fact, it was built *out of* English soil. A mound of soil (called a motte, from the French word for 'mound') was piled up, the top was flattened and a wooden tower was built on top. At the foot of the mound was a large area (the bailey) with buildings, all enclosed by an earthen rampart. Within a year a second motte-and-bailey castle, Baile Hill, was built in York, on the other side of the River Ouse.

Both of York's Norman castles were put up as a show of force. Neither the town nor the county had seen anything like them before. Their purpose was simple enough – obvious signs of Norman power and control over the local population.

---

1. It's sometimes claimed to be the first Norman castle built in England. However, a few Norman-style castles were already here, such as at Ewyas Harold, Herefordshire, built by a Norman in the 1040s. The Normans also brought pre-built wooden castles with them in 1066 and the first of these 'flat packs' was put up at Pevensey, Sussex.

Castles and Cathedrals

Motte-and-bailey castles were soon appearing across Yorkshire. Many mottes, like the two in York, can still be seen today. There are other good examples at Mexborough, Laughton-en-le-Morthen, Thorne and Bradfield, South Yorkshire.

Massacre at the castle

On the night of 16 March 1190, a mob set fire to York Castle. Inside was the town's Jewish community, the largest outside London. They had sought refuge in the castle after an outbreak of anti-Jewish feeling that had swept the land that year.

As many as one hundred and fifty Jews may have died. Some took their own lives; others surrendered and were then murdered.

The massacre is one of the bleakest and saddest events in York's history.

Yorkshire A Very Peculiar History

Castles made of stone

For some of Yorkshire's castles, a motte-and-bailey was just the beginning. In time, their timber towers were replaced by castles built of solid stone. This happened at York Castle in 1245, when the wooden tower on top of the motte was replaced with a stone tower. It was originally known as the King's Tower, but its name was eventually changed to Clifford's Tower, either after Roger de Clifford, a prisoner executed there in 1322, or perhaps after Henry Clifford, Earl of Cumberland, who was in command of troops there in the 1600s (most people pick the first option).

On the oposite page are some of Yorkshire's other notable stone castles.

Skipton Castle, North Yorkshire. It began as a Norman motte-and-bailey castle, and was eventually rebuilt in stone. Today, it is one of the most complete and best preserved medieval castles in England.

Scarborough Castle, East Yorkshire. Perched on the cliffs are the ruins of what was once one of Britain's strongest castles. King Henry II (reigned 1154-89) and his son, King John (reigned 1199-1216), added walls and towers to the castle, turning it into a royal fortress.

Richmond Castle, North Yorkshire. The first castle was built in 1071 by Alan Rufus ('the Red'), William the Conqueror's cousin.[1] In the late 1100s a stone keep was built, with walls 3.4 m (11 ft) thick. It is one of Britain's oldest stone keeps, and one of the best.

Conisbrough Castle, South Yorkshire. It has the country's best Norman circular keep (the strongest part of a castle, where the owner lived). The castle was built in the 1180s out of Yorkshire magnesian limestone – the same type of stone used to build York Minster. The keep still stands to almost its full height (about 29.5 m / 97 ft).

Pontefract Castle, West Yorkshire. From its origins as a Norman motte-and-bailey, built on land given to one of William the Conqueror's trusted men, the castle was rebuilt in stone on a grand scale in the 1200s. In its prime, it was a major fortress, and one of the strongest castles in Britain.

---

1. *William gave Rufus a vast amount of land. He owned 250,000 acres in Yorkshire, Norfolk, Suffolk, Northamptonshire, Cambridgeshire and London. He died in 1089, leaving an estate valued at £11,000. In 2007, it was estimated this was equivalent to £81 billion, making Alan Rufus the richest man ever to have lived in Britain!*

Secret tunnels under Richmond Castle

There are said to be secret tunnels under Richmond Castle, and there are legends to go with them.

Little drummer boy

A drummer boy was sent down to explore a tunnel, beating his drum as he went. Soldiers listened for the drum beats and plotted the course of the tunnel as it headed out of town towards Easby Abbey. But then the drumming suddenly stopped, and the little drummer boy was never seen or heard from again. The Drummer Boy Stone marks the spot where the drumming was last heard.

King Arthur and his knights

Mr Thompson, a local potter, went down into a tunnel and found King Arthur asleep with his knights. Nearby were a sword and a horn. As he was about to blow the horn the knights started to wake – and the frightened potter fled back to the surface.

Five Things You Didn't Know About Yorkshire Castles

1. In 1596, Robert Redhead, jailer at York Castle, was caught selling building stone. He'd got it by knocking down parts of the castle! He was hanged, of course.

2. York Castle was also a mint where gold and silver coins were made, a court house and a prison.

3. Pontefract Castle sealed its place in English history in 1400, when the deposed King Richard II (reigned 1377-99) was imprisoned and died there. *"Hack'd to death"*, according to William Shakespeare in his play *Richard III*; others say he starved to death.

4. Another monarch imprisoned in a Yorkshire castle was Mary, Queen of Scots, who spent most of 1568 at Bolton Castle, together with thirty of her knights and six ladies-in-waiting. Rugs and furniture were borrowed from local houses and from Barnard Castle, County Durham, to make the castle feel fit for a queen.

5. At the top of the keep at Conisbrough Castle was a pigeon loft, at the bottom a dungeon.

Yorkshire A Very Peculiar History

Cathedrals

If York is the crown of Yorkshire, then York Minster[1] is its jewel. But it's not the only cathedral in Yorkshire – the county has four more:

Bradford	Cathedral and Parish Church of St Peter
Ripon	The Cathedral Church of St Peter and St Wilfrid
Sheffield	The Cathedral of St Peter and St Paul
Wakefield	The Cathedral Church of All Saints
York	The Cathedral and Metropolitan Church of St Peter

A cathedral is the most important church in a bishop's diocese – the geographical area over which he has authority.

---

1. *Churches known as 'minsters' are generally ones founded in the Anglo-Saxon period as teaching churches. Their purpose was to teach and spread Christianity in their area. Yorkshire has two minster churches – the cathedral in York and the parish church at Beverley, East Yorkshire. Beverley Minster is regarded as the most impressive church in England that is not a cathedral.*

York Minster

Let the facts about this great building speak for themselves:

160 m (525 ft) long, that's longer than 1 ½ football pitches.

76 m (249 ft) wide, wider than a Boeing 747's wingspan.

27 m (88.5 ft) high from floor to ceiling – that's as big as 5 double-decker buses stacked on top of each other!

At **56 m (184 ft)** high, the West Towers are taller than Nelson's Column.

At **71 m (233 ft)** high, Central Tower is even taller.

275 steps to climb to the top of Central Tower.

128 stained-glass windows with two million pieces of glass.

250 years to complete construction.

Yorkshire A Very Peculiar History

And now its history...

York Minster traces its origins right the way back to Anglian (Anglo-Saxon) times – almost 1,400 years ago – when a wooden church was built for the baptism of King Edwin of Northumbria in AD 627 (see page 46). No one knows where this first church stood, as all traces of it disappeared long ago.

The first stone church to stand on the site was built as early as AD 640, and dedicated to St Peter. It served the community for some four hundred years until, in 1069, it was destroyed during the Norman Conquest of England.

In 1080, work started on building a new church in the Norman style of architecture. Its walls reused chunks of masonry robbed from the city's ancient Roman buildings. The rough stone was plastered over and painted white with red lines, to give the appearance of neat blocks of cut stone. The Norman church lasted for around two hundred years, until the 1220s when it was cleared away to build an even bigger church – the present-day Minster. All that survives of the Norman Minster is the crypt, which is under the

Castles and Cathedrals

building. Built in the Gothic style of architecture, the Minster as seen today took about two hundred and fifty years to complete. It was put up in stages, and was finally completed in 1472.

It's a wonder York Minster is still here, as there have been at least ten serious fires in the building's long history.

Year	Firestarter
741	The first known fire: cause unknown.
866	The Vikings capture York and burn the Minster.
1069	The Normans burn the Minster, during the Harrying of the North.
1079	The Vikings are back, and burn the Minster again.
1137	Another fire: cause unknown.
1463	Same again: cause unknown.
1753	The roof is releaded and catches fire from the builders' hot coals.
1829	Jonathan Martin, arsonist, burns the Minster (he spends the rest of his life in a hospital for the insane).
1840	A candle causes a fire.
1984	Lightning strikes the Minster and causes a massive fire in the roof.

Ten Things You Didn't Know About York Minster

1. The Minster's twelve bells have 479,001,600 different musical combinations or changes. To ring a full peal takes four to four and a half hours and involves 5,088 changes rung in strict order without repeats.

2. York Minster has over 200 carved stone grotesques and gargoyles adorning the exterior, depicting a wide range of imaginative and sometimes humorous figures and creatures. One recent addition is a carving of a person sipping from a pint glass, a nod to York's pub culture. In 2018, a stonemason carved a grotesque figure inspired by her father, complete with a Nike swoosh on his medieval boot!

3. The York Minster Library is England's largest cathedral library, with more than 120,000 books and pamphlets, including Charles I's prayer book, donated in 1633.

4. The Minster is the only cathedral in Britain with its own private police force. A team of nine or ten police patrol the cathedral day and night.

5. The Minster's 'Great Peter' bell is the fourth heaviest bell in Britain (10.8 tons). It's part of a clock, and strikes the hour with the deepest note of any bell in Britain.

6. The Minster has a dragon! Halfway down the nave, high up on the wall, is a dragon carved in stone. It was probably used as a lifting point to raise a heavy font lid in medieval times.

7. The Minster has mice! Its kneeling desks were carved in wood by Robert Thompson (1876-1955) of Kilburn, North Yorkshire. He was known as 'the Mouseman of Kilburn', or just 'the Mouseman', because he carved a tiny mouse on to each piece of furniture he made.

8. The Minster is the only Cathedral in Britain that puts mistletoe as well as holly on its altar at Christmas. Mistletoe has ancient Pagan associations with protection and healing and is a pre-Christian tradition.

9. The Minster's Great East Window, made between 1405 and 1408, is the single largest area of medieval glass in the world (about the size of a tennis court).

10. The Minster lost the South Transept roof in a fire in 1984. It was rebuilt, and viewers of the BBC TV programme *Blue Peter* designed six of the new roof bosses (carvings) that decorate the ceiling. The programme held a competition to design bosses showing significant events in the twentieth century. The winning bosses show man on the moon, saving the whale, fire in the south transept, famine relief, raising the *Mary Rose* and the conquest of space.

Oi! You down there! No shirking!

Peasants had to earn their keep, but lords and kings could simply have one built.

Chapter Seven

Poor Peasants and Mean Monks

Yorkshire in the Middle Ages must have seemed like a county of contrasts - a place where war and peace existed side by side.

The evidence for this is written into the county's landscape. On the one hand, are signs of its violent past, from mighty castles to battlefields, and on the other are the county's monasteries - abbeys and priories where monks and nuns devoted their lives to peaceful prayer. But this period in Yorkshire's history isn't only a story about grand buildings, powerful barons and greedy abbots. It's also a tale about plague and vanished villages, and how these have also left their mark.

Yorkshire A Very Peculiar History

Britain's baddest years

The 1300s were bad for Britain, and bad for Yorkshire. Bad because:

- Harvests failed across the land.
- Sheep and cattle died of disease.
- Scottish armies raided northern England and ransacked the Yorkshire towns of Northallerton and Knaresborough.
- Storms lashed the east coast of Yorkshire, causing rivers to flood and washing land and villages clean away.

But the worst was yet to come, and when it did, nowhere was spared from the killer plague known as the Black Death.

Rats: the tiny troublemakers of the 14th century!

Poor Peasants and Mean Monks

The Black Death in Yorkshire

The Black Death[1] arrived in England in 1348, and the bad news spread fast. On 28 July that year, William Zouche, Archbishop of York, sent a warning to his flock. He said:

"Everybody knows, since the news is now widely spread, what great pestilence, mortality and infection of the air there are in divers parts of the world and which, at this moment are threatening in particular the land of England."

The Archbishop told people to pray, but a fat lot of good it did them. The plague spread north, and reached Yorkshire in the spring of 1349.

There was no cure for the painful boils and buboes[2] that blistered and bubbled up under the skin, the non-stop throwing up, the coughing, the fever or the aching bones. Death was inevitable.

---

1. 'It wasn't called the Black Death at the time. Instead, people referred to it as the 'Great Pestilence' or the 'Great Plague' - that's 'great' as in 'immense', not 'great' as in 'excellent'. It got the name 'Black Death' in the 1500s, when writers described the plague's dreadful effect it had on society.
2. Swellings

Yorkshire A Very Peculiar History

It's hard to say how many people died of plague in Yorkshire, as accurate records were not made. The county might not have been as hard hit as neighbouring Lincolnshire, which was ravaged, but countless thousands were seen off by the pestilence. The dead were quickly buried, sometimes in mass graves known as plague pits.

One fact is known for certain – the plague spared No one, not even the clergy. Across Yorkshire, about 220 parish priests died. This was almost half the total number of priests.

At Meaux Abbey, near Beverley, East Yorkshire, the monks felt the ground tremble beneath their feet. It was, they decided, an omen of the horror to come. The full force of the plague descended upon them in the summer of 1349, killing the Abbot, Hugh de Leven, and five monks in a single day, Wednesday, 12 August. Out of the community of forty-two monks, thirty-two perished and only ten survived. It was almost a total wipeout, from which the abbey never fully recovered.

Poor Peasants and Mean Monks

As for the town of Hull, it was dealt a double blow. If the plague didn't kill off the population, the floods did, as the Hull and Humber rivers both burst their banks, swamping the town and the surrounding countryside.

By the time the Black Death had run its course, as much as half the population of England had died from it. No one knows the exact figure, but some three million people are thought to have been bumped off by the Great Pestilence.

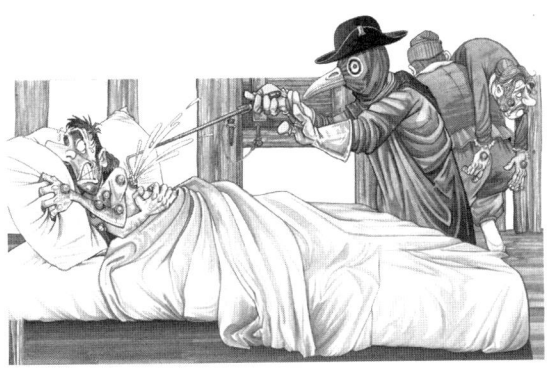

The plague doctor was a bit of a quack.

Yorkshire A Very Peculiar History

Vanished villages

As a direct consequence of the Black Death, towns and villages across England went into decline. There were fewer people around, buildings fell into decay and farm land was left to go to waste.

In York, a lack of stonemasons brought building work on the Minster to a stop on the west front and the nave. No further work was done until 1361.

In the most severe cases, villages were left abandoned. They're called deserted medieval villages, or DMVs for short.

There are around 3,000 known DMVs in England, and Yorkshire has at least 425, which is more than ten per cent of the national total.

Poor Peasants and Mean Monks

Wharram Percy – top DMV and original zombie fighters

The lost village of Wharram Percy[1], about 10 km (6 miles) north of Malton, North Yorkshire, is England's best-known deserted medieval village (DMV). This fame comes from forty years of archaeological excavations, from 1952 to 1992, making it the longest dig in British history.

The Wharram Percy dig unveiled the village's peak in the 1100s, revealing two manor houses, two corn mills, a church, and 35 small wooden houses. Beyond the houses villagers grew predominantly cereal crops.

More recently, human bones from the site showed evidence of ancient practices to stop corpses from rising from their graves and spreading disease. Knife marks were found mostly in the head and neck area, along with evidence of burning body parts and deliberate breaking of bones after death, presumably to prevent them from coming back to life.

---

1. 'Wharram' means 'place by the pots', from an Old English (Anglo-Saxon) word for pot, cauldron or kettle. 'Percy' indicates the village was originally owned by the Percy family.

Yorkshire A Very Peculiar History

Wharram Percy was a typical English medieval village but, like so many others, it became a victim of changing times.

The Black Death certainly visited the village and wiped out some of the people, but it wasn't the plague that killed Wharram Percy. Instead, its downfall was due to changes in farming.

By the 1400s, some landlords realised there was more money to be made from sheep farming than cereal farming. The landlord of Wharram Percy was one of them, and he started to evict his tenants and convert their arable fields to grass for sheep to graze.

By 1458, the village had shrunk to just sixteen houses, and by 1517 the last of the villagers was forced to leave and find new homes elsewhere. From then on, Wharram Percy was a deserted village. Its flimsy houses fell or were pulled down, until all that remained was its stone church dedicated to St Martin. The church carried on serving the surrounding parish, and the last service was held there as late as 1949.

Five Things You Didn't Know About the Black Death in Yorkshire

1. William Zouche, the Archbishop of York, was kept busy by the Black Death. So many bodies were being buried, new graveyards were needed, and it was his job to consecrate them all (make them into holy ground). He also had to keep asking the Pope for permission to ordinate extra clergy, as the plague was killing them off so fast.

2. Eleven graveyards were specially set aside for the burial of victims of the Black Death, eight of them in North Yorkshire.

3. The villages of Rotmanby, East Yorkshire, and Barthorpe, North Yorkshire, ceased to exist as their entire populations seem to have been killed off by the plague.

4. A burial pit at St Mary's Church, Leake, North Yorkshire, was filled with the bones of about 500 people. It may have been a plague pit, where the dead were quickly buried.

5. Doncaster was very badly affected, with as many as six out of every ten people dying of plague.

Yorkshire A Very Peculiar History

Robin Hood – a Yorkshire outlaw

Warning: if you are from Nottinghamshire, you might like to skip the next few pages.

In the tale of *Robin Hood and Guy of Gisborne*, the hero says: "*My name is Robin Hood of Barnesdale*". That would be Barnsdale, South Yorkshire. It's one of the oldest of the Robin Hood tales, and dates from at least 1475. The tale describes the exploits of a Yorkshire outlaw called Robin Hood who stuck up for the poor during the 13th or 14th centuries.

Robin Hood, doing what he does best – giving to the poor.

Poor Peasants and Mean Monks

Here are some of the reasons why Yorkshire folk claim Robin Hood as one of their own:

1. The York link
The earliest mention of an outlaw called Robin Hood is from York Assizes on 25 July 1225. This man was a *real* Robin Hood, not a legend. Could all the legends about Robin Hood be based on this man?

2. The Barnsdale link
The earliest tales about Robin Hood are set in and around Barnsdale, near Doncaster, South Yorkshire.

3. The Loxley link
Again, the earliest tales link Robin Hood to a Yorkshire place – Loxley, near Sheffield, South Yorkshire. The tales say he was born there.

4. The Kirklees link
As for Robin Hood's death, it's claimed he was killed and buried at Kirklees Priory, Mirfield, West Yorkshire.

Yorkshire's Robin Hood (and Little John) places

To show just how much Robin Hood is rated in Yorkshire, here are some of the many places named after him and his Merry Men:

- Robin Hood's Well, near Skelbrooke, South Yorkshire.

- Robin Hood's Stone, near to Robin Hood's Well, but long since disappeared.

- Robin Hood's Wood, near Fountains Abbey, North Yorkshire.

- Robin Hood's Bay, North Yorkshire.

- Robin Hood, an area of Wakefield, West Yorkshire (home of Robin Hood Athletic football team, the Robin Hood Watersports centre, and Robin Hood Primary School).

- Little John's Well, which can be found in woodland at Hampole, South Yorkshire.[1]

---

1. Little John was a fellow outlaw of Robin Hood, and was said to be Robin's second-in-command of the Merry Men.

Poor Peasants and Mean Monks

Magnificent monasteries

Yorkshire has the finest collection of medieval monasteries in Britain. Selby Abbey, North Yorkshire, is the oldest monastery in the county. It was founded in 1069, during the reign of William the Conqueror, and was the first monastery to be opened in the north after the Norman Conquest. Many more were to follow until, by the 1500s, the number had increased to about one hundred, each with a community of monks and lay workers (non-religious people).

In date order

Monastery	Founded
Selby Abbey	1069
Kirkham Priory	1120
Fountains Abbey	1132
Rievaulx Abbey	1132
Byland Abbey	1135
Kirkstall Abbey	1152
Bolton Priory	1154
Monk Bretton Priory	154
Jervaulx Abbey	1156
Coverham Abbey	1190

Yorkshire A Very Peculiar History

The troubles of the world must have seemed far away, and for almost five hundred years all was well with Britain's monasteries.

In Yorkshire, the monks lived quiet lives in secluded parts of the county, their monasteries prospered, they acquired large amounts of land and the buildings grew into magnificent structures with expensive stained-glass windows and ornately tiled floors.

In fact, the monasteries ended up owning more than a quarter of all the farm land in England. That made them powerful and important landowners. The monks rented the land out to the country's farmers, and that's how the monasteries became rich. Is it any wonder that monks – who had given up worldy goods – were accused of being mean and greedy landlords?

As for what happened to them, and to their magnificent monasteries, flick to Chapter 9.

Five Things You Didn't Know About Yorkshire's Monasteries

1. The monks of Jervaulx[1] Abbey, North Yorkshire, are said to have invented the recipe for Wensleydale cheese, which they made with milk from their large flocks of sheep.

2. At Bolton Priory, the Clapham family of Beamsley, North Yorkshire, were buried in upright positions. The poet William Wordsworth described it as a 'grisly sight'.

3. Fountains Abbey, North Yorkshire, is Britain's largest monastic ruin and a World Heritage Site.

4. The monks of Rievaulx Abbey, North Yorkshire, farmed 14,000 sheep and sold their wool to cloth merchants from Flanders, France and Italy.

5. Kirkham Priory, North Yorkshire, was used as a top-secret base for troops training for the D-Day landings in Normandy, France, in 1944.

The White Rose

House of York

The Red Rose

House of Lancaster

Chapter Eight

The Bloody Roses

Yorkshire is the White Rose county, and somewhere to the west of it (Yorkshirefolk seem strangely vague about a precise location) is the Red Rose county of Lancashire.

Two counties, two roses, one bitter power struggle, and only one winner. That, in a nutshell, sums up the rivalry between the House of York and the House of Lancaster, which dragged them into a civil war known as the Wars of the Roses. It was a contest to decide which of them had the right to the throne of England.

Yorkshire A Very Peculiar History

So what's with the roses?

It was a certain well-known playwright, William Shakespeare, who, in his play *Henry VI*, written in about 1590, had the rival dukes of York and Lancaster picking white and red roses in a garden. It's a dramatic scene in the play, but totally made up by Mr Shakespeare.

And then there's the name itself, 'Wars of the Roses'. It's very catchy, but it's also an invention, this time by the author Sir Walter Scott. He came up with it for a book he wrote in 1819, called *Ivanhoe*, and repeated it ten years later in another book, *Anne of Geierstein*.

So what's the truth behind the thorny problem of the roses, and the white rose in particular?

The fact is, the White Rose of York is older than the bust-up between Yorkshire and Lancashire. The so-called Wars began in 1455 but, according to tradition[1], Yorkshire had already picked a white rose as its emblem long before the two sides fell out with each other. The story goes that

---

1. *A bluffer's way of saying 'no one really knows, but it's what everyone thinks happened'.*

The Bloody Roses

it was Edmund of Langley (1341-1402), the first Duke of York, who chose a pure white rose (the dog rose, or *Rosa alba*) as the official emblem of the House of York.

Edmund was a descendant of King Edward I (reigned 1272-1307) whose symbol was a golden rose. To show he had links to the English monarchy, Edmund decided to use a rose as his badge, just like the king. He couldn't use gold as this was the king's colour, so he chose white.[1]

By the time Edmund's grandson, Richard Plantagenet, became the third Duke of York in 1425, the symbol of a white rose for Yorkshire was firmly fixed in the minds of Yorkshirefolk, and that's the way it has stayed ever since.

The white rose may have been chosen long ago as a symbol of innocence and purity, but today, to Yorkshirefolk the world over, it means just one thing: home, sweet home.

---

1. *The House of Lancaster was also related to the monarchy, and they also took a rose for their badge, which they coloured red.*

Which way up?

From the earliest days, way back in the 1400s, the White Rose of Yorkshire has been shown with five petals separated by barbs or sepals. The big question is, should it be shown with a petal or a barb at the top?

Petal at top

Barb at top

There seems to be no right (or wrong) answer, and you will see the rose shown both ways, and even halfway between the two!

Petal and barb at top

The Bloody Roses

Let battle commence!

If anyone should get the blame for starting the Wars of the Roses, it should probably be King Henry VI (reigned 1422-61 and 1470-71). Henry was from the House of Lancaster. He was a weak king who was easily influenced by the nobles at his court. The nobles were from England's two leading families – the houses of Lancaster and York. They were bitter rivals.

In 1453, King Henry became too ill to rule England, and that's when things started to get out of hand. At the time of his illness, the king had no children. That meant there was no heir to pass control of England to while he was ill. This placed the ruling House of Lancaster in a difficult situation. Someone had to rule the country during the king's illness, but who? Step forward Richard Plantagenet, the Duke of York.

The Duke of York was technically the next in line to the throne. He was a warrior, he was rich, and he had a lot of important friends. The problem was, Richard came from the other side – the House of York. And, to make matters worse, he

Yorkshire A Very Peculiar History

had powerful enemies who had befriended poor old King Henry.

When King Henry fell ill, the Duke of York seized the moment. It was his chance to take control of England, and take what he thought was rightfully his. He was asking for trouble, and he knew it. Very soon, England's leading families had taken sides. They either supported the House of York or the House of Lancaster.

But then King Henry did two things that complicated the situation for the Duke of York.

First, Henry produced a son, Edward (known as Edward of Lancaster). That meant he now had an heir. Great news for the House of Lancaster, but bad news for the House of York.

Second, Henry recovered from his illness, got better, and took over the reigns of power once again. Cheers all round from the Lancastrian supporters, groans from the Yorkists.

The two sides were at such odds with each other it was inevitable they would end up fighting. King Henry asked the Duke of York to meet

The Bloody Roses

him, but the Duke refused. Instead, he gathered an army and marched towards London. He reached St Albans, just north of the capital, where he was met by a Lancastrian army. The sides clashed on 22 May 1455. It was a decisive Yorkist victory.

COME ON, YOU REDS!

Talk about a rose between two thorns!

The Lancastrians were a proud and rowdy bunch.

Yorkshire A Very Peculiar History

This battle was over, but the Wars of the Roses had only just begun, and seventeen more battles were to follow. For the next thirty years, civil war raged between the House of York and the House of Lancaster.

Yorkshire battles

As a result of the Battle of St Albans, the Lancastrians declared the Yorkists to be traitors. Each side called on its supporters to rise up and fight the other, and the battles they fought were among the fiercest ever seen on British soil. Two of the conflict's major battles were fought in Yorkshire – the Battle of Wakefield (1460) and the Battle of Towton (1461).

Battle of Wakefield

Date	30 December 1460
Location	Wakefield, West Yorkshire
Yorkists	5,000
Lancastrians	15,000
Killed: York	700–2,500
Killed: Lancaster	200
Result	Lancastrian victory

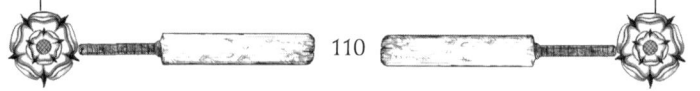

Which side were they on?

Don't think of the Wars of the Roses as a series of battles between the counties of Yorkshire and Lancashire: they weren't.

The battle lines were not drawn as if they were lines on a map. Instead, the Wars of the Roses were fought between the supporters of the two sides – and Yorkshire folk were just as divided as everyone else in England.

Yorkshire families who supported the House of York:

- The Nevilles of Sheriff Hutton
- The Scropes of Bolton
- The Latimers of Danby
- The Mowbrays of Thirsk

Yorkshire families who supported the House of Lancaster:

- The Percys of Wressle
- The Cliffords of Skipton
- The Ros of Helmsley
- The Greystocks of Hinderskelfe
- The Staffords of Holderness
- The Talbots of Sheffield

Off with his head!

Richard Plantagenet, the third Duke of York, never did become king of England. He'd got close to the throne, but it was always just beyond his grasp. The Battle of Wakefield turned out to be his last stand against the Lancastrian forces intent on destroying him.

For some reason, which to this day remains a mystery, Richard headed out from the safety of his stronghold at Sandal Castle, on the edge of Wakefield, to face the Lancastrians.

Perhaps Richard misjudged the strength of the opposition; perhaps he feared being starved during a siege of his castle.

Richard was outnumbered, and although he could have waited for reinforcements to arrive, he chose to meet his enemy in battle – and paid the ultimate price. According to tradition, he died fighting, with his back to a stand of willow trees.

However, an account, written at the time, says he was captured alive and then executed:

The Bloody Roses

"They stood him [the Duke of York] on a little anthill and placed on his head, as if a crown, a vile garland made of reeds, just as the Jews did to the Lord, and bent the knee to him, saying in jest, 'Hail King, without rule. Hail King, without ancestry, Hail leader and prince, with almost no subjects or possessions'. And having said this and various other shameful and dishonourable things to him, at last they cut off his head."

Another account says that Richard's head was taken to the city of York where it was fixed to a pole at Micklegate Bar, one of the gateways into the city. A paper crown was placed on its head, in mockery of the gold crown of England that Richard had sought in vain.

Battle of Towton

Date	29 March 1461
Location	Towton, North Yorkshire
Yorkists	20,000-36,000
Lancastrians	25,000-42,000
Killed: York	5,000-12,000
Killed: Lancaster	8,000-20,000
Result	Yorkist victory

The first Yorkist king

Three months after the death of Richard, Yorkshire witnessed the bloodiest battle ever fought in Britain. It was payback time for the Yorkists, who inflicted a crushing defeat on the Lancastrians at the Battle of Towton.

It was fought in a snowstorm on Palm Sunday 1461. The Yorkists were led by Edward Plantagenet, the fourth Duke of York (he had inherited the title after the death of his father, Richard). An estimated 50,000 men clashed between the villages of Saxton and Towton, North Yorkshire.

The Bloody Roses

Edward declared that no mercy should be shown to the Lancastrians, and at nine o'clock in the morning, the battle began. Snow blew into the faces of the Lancastrian archers, who couldn't see where to fire their arrows. To make matters worse, the Yorkists picked up the Lancastrians' arrows and fired them back.

By mid-afternoon, the Yorkists were in trouble. But the arrival of reinforcements turned the battle in their favour, and the Lancastrians fled. Thousands were cut down, and many drowned as they tried to cross the River Wharfe and Cock Beck stream. In a final act of revenge, the rotting head of Richard, Duke of York, was taken down from York's Micklegate Bar, and in its place went the heads of defeated Lancastrians. Later that year, Edward, Duke of York, was crowned King Edward IV, and he became the first Yorkist king (reigned 1461–70 and 1471–83).

Ten Things You Didn't Know About the Wars of the Roses in Yorkshire

1. The Battle of Wakefield could be the source of the mnemonic for remembering the colours of the rainbow: 'Richard Of York Gave Battle In Vain' (Red, Orange, Yellow, Green, Blue, Indigo, Violet).

2. The place where Richard, Duke of York, is said to have fallen in the Battle of Wakefield is commemorated today by a monument in the grounds of Manygates Education Centre, Wakefield. The stone statue of Richard has long since lost its head – just as the real Richard did in 1460.

3. Sir Richard Neville fought on the side of the Yorkists at the Battle of Wakefield. He was captured and taken to Pontefract, where he was lynched by the mob. His head was stuck on a pole at York, next to the head of Richard, Duke of York.

4. Neither side emerged as clear winners in the Battle of Ferrybridge, West Yorkshire, fought on 28 March 1461. It was a draw.

5. At the Battle of Towton, it was said that the stream known as Cock Beck could be crossed without getting your feet wet, by stepping on the bodies of drowned Lancastrians.

6. The dead from the Battle of Towton were buried in mass graves on the battlefield. In 1463, King Richard III ordered their reburial in Saxton churchyard.

7. Lord Dacre, a Lancastrian, was killed at the Battle of Towton. His tomb is in Saxton churchyard. Legend says he was buried standing upright alongside his horse.

8. In 1996, builders working at Towton Hall found a burial pit containing the skeletons of about fifty men who died during the Battle of Towton. They had been killed by swords, knives, billhooks[1] and war hammers.

9. The skeletons found at Towton Hall are thought to be the remains of Lancastrians. Some skulls had scratch marks on the sides, possibly from having their ears cut off as battle trophies.

10. Of the eighteen battles fought in the Wars of the Roses, the final score was:

House of York	11
House of Lancaster	6
Drawn	1

1. A long, spear type of weapon, like a pike or a halberd

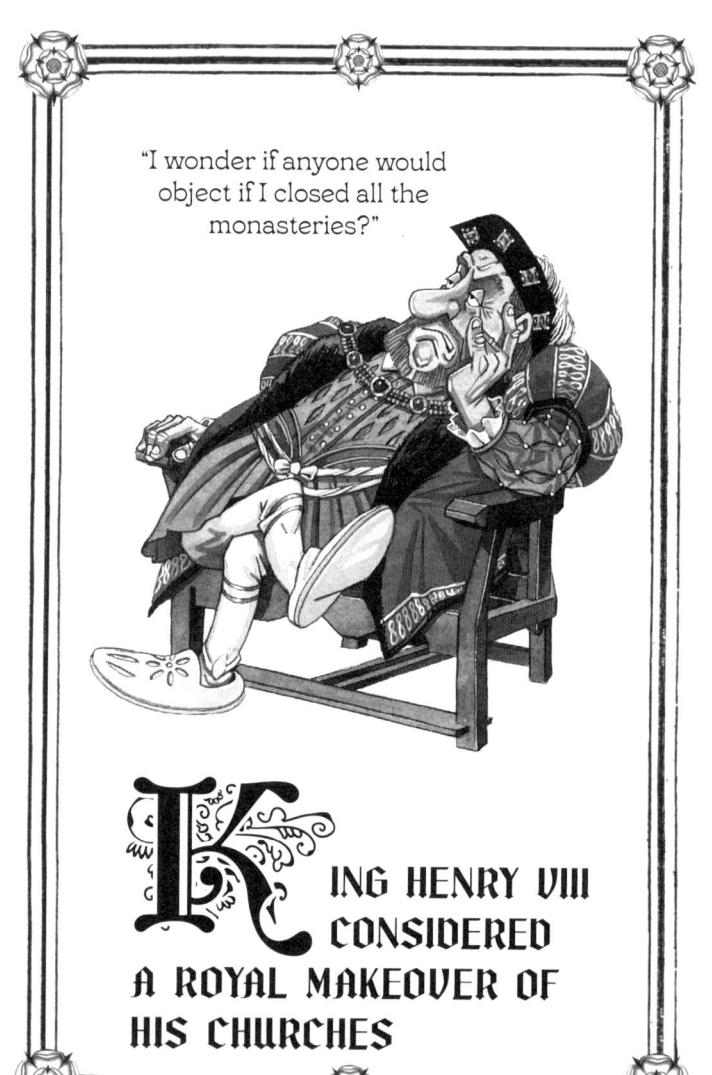

Chapter Nine

Oi, Henry! Hands off!

When Henry VIII became king in 1509, there were about one hundred monasteries in Yorkshire. They'd been there for centuries, and were as much a part of the landscape as castles, cathedrals and parish churches.

However, little did the monks and nuns know, but time was running out for them and their magnificent monasteries. King Henry had a quarrel, and then he had a plan to rid the nation of all its abbeys, friaries, priories and nunneries.

Yorkshire A Very Peculiar History

At the start of his reign, Henry accepted the monasteries as part of everyday English life. But, when he fell out with the Catholic Church, who refused to allow him to divorce his queen, Catherine of Aragon, Henry turned his anger on the Church.

He set about closing the monasteries down and confiscating their land and possessions. Henry's revenge, which began in 1536, became known as the Dissolution of the Monasteries.[1]

Monks and nuns were evicted from their homes. Their land, buildings and other possessions - farm animals, crops, books, church clothing, pots and pans, and so on - were seized on behalf of the king.

However, for a time it looked as if Henry's grand plan was going to fail, due to a northern resistance movement that had Yorkshire at its heart.

---

1. *About 650 monasteries were closed during Henry's Dissolution of the Monasteries. The last one to close its doors was Waltham Abbey, Essex, closed by Henry in 1540.*

Pilgrimage of Grace

The rebellion against Henry began in Lincolnshire in early October 1536, and quickly spread to neighbouring Yorkshire, where Robert Aske (c.1500-37), a lawyer from Aughton, near Selby, East Yorkshire, became the rebels' leader. Aske described Yorkshire's monasteries as "one of the beauties of this realm to all men and strangers passing through", and the last thing he wanted was to see them closed down. It was a popular uprising, and Aske soon had a large force of 'pilgrims' who pledged to defend the monasteries. Aske led about 10,000 pilgrims to York, and it was this march that gave the rebellion its name - the Pilgrimage of Grace. Once in York, Aske issued a proclamation which said:

"For thys pylgrymage we have taken hyt for the presevacyon of Crystes churche, of thys realme of England, the kynge our soverayne lorde, the nobylytie and comyns of the same, and to the entent to macke petycion to the kinges highnes for the reformacyon of that whyche is amysse within thys hys realme."[1]

---

1. In plain English, "Oi, Henry! Hands off!"

Yorkshire A Very Peculiar History

Most of Yorkshire's leading families took the side of the rebels. From York, Aske advanced to Pontefract Castle, which he took after a short siege on 20 October. Sheltering inside was Edward Lee, the Archbishop of York, who agreed to join the rebels (the Archbishop later changed his mind and switched over to the king's side).

By the end of October, the rebellion had spread across northern England, from Yorkshire to the Scottish border. But then it was all over, as quickly as it had started.

Aske was arrested in 1537 and taken to the Tower of London. He was found guilty of high treason and taken back to York, where he was dragged through the city streets on a hurdle (a type of frame), then hanged in chains outside Clifford's Tower as a warning to anyone else who dared to question the king's authority.

Hanged holy men

It wasn't only the leaders of the rebellion who were executed – the heads of some Yorkshire monasteries met the same fate.

- William Thirsk, Abbot of Fountains Abbey
  – hanged in London

- Adam Sedbergh, Abbot of Jervaulx Abbey
  – hanged in London

- William Trafford, Abbot of Sawley Abbey[1]
  – hanged in Lancaster Castle

- William Wood, Prior of Bridlington Priory
  – hanged in London

- James Cockerell, Prior of Guisborough Priory
  – hanged in London

1. In present-day Lancashire, but until 1974 it was in Yorkshire.

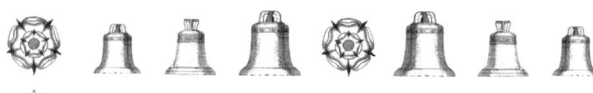

Adam Sedbergh woz 'ere

Adam Sedbergh was the last Abbot of Jervaulx Abbey. He was imprisoned in the Tower of London, and carved his name on the wall of his cell:

ADAM SEDBAR. ABBAS JOREVALL 1537

- Hanged at Tyburn, 2 June 1537.
- His head was put on London Bridge.

Going, going, gone!

With the rebels dealt with, King Henry pressed on with the matter of closing down the monasteries. It was business as usual.

By 1540 Yorkshire was a monastery-free zone. From then on, some of the finest buildings in Britain became quarries and scrapyards.

Oi, Henry! Hands off!

Monasteries were sold off to private buyers, who set about dismantling them piece by piece. Their stone and timber were carted away and the lead was stripped from the roofs – all to be reused and recycled.

- At Kirkstall Abbey, near Leeds, West Yorkshire, the bronze bells were smashed and the metal was recast as cannon. Some of the stone was used to make a bridge.

- Whitby Abbey was sold to Richard Cholmley who used some of its stone to build himself a mansion.

- When the monks of Fountains Abbey, near Ripon, North Yorkshire, were forced to leave, their 1,976 horned cattle, 1,146 sheep, 86 horses, 79 pigs and 221 quarters of grain (2.8 tons) were sold to Sir Richard Gresham, the Lord Mayor of London.

Yorkshire A Very Peculiar History

The end of Roche Abbey

On 23 June 1538, Abbot Henry Cundall (1531-8), the Abbot of Roche Abbey[1], near Maltby, South Yorkshire, and his seventeen monks gathered in the abbey's chapter house.

He was handed a legal document by Henry VIII's commissioners. With a flourish of his quill he signed it, and Roche Abbey was handed over to the king.

In return for surrendering the abbey, each monk was granted a pension. The Abbot received £33 6s 8d (£33.33) for his pension, and was allowed to keep his "*books, the fourth part of the plate, cattle, household items, a chalice, vestment and a portion of corn*".

Roche Abbey was then destroyed to prevent the monks from coming back.

---

1. 'Roche' is French for 'rock'. According to a legend, the abbey got its name when Durand, the first Abbot (1147-59), was wandering along the Maltby Beck with twelve followers when he found "hewn out upon a rock, by God's own hand, an image of our Saviour on the Cross!" The abbey was built close to where this miraculous sign in the rock was found.

Oi, Henry! Hands off!

The destruction of Roche Abbey is well known to historians, thanks to Michael Sherbrook. He was a priest at nearby Wickersley, and wrote a detailed account of the abbey's fate.

According to Sherbrook this is what happened at Roche Abbey:

- The church was spoiled first.
- The wooden seats of the choir were burned to melt the lead on the church roof.
- Tombs were shattered.
- Pewter vessels were stolen.
- The abbot's lodging, the monks' dormitory, the refectory, the cloister and all the other buildings within the abbey walls were vandalised.
- Oddly, the abbey's ox-houses and pig-houses were not touched by the looters.

As Sherbrook put it:
"...it seemed that every person was intent upon filching and spoiling what he could."

Closed until further notice

About one hundred and twenty religious institutions of all kinds were closed in Yorkshire during the Dissolution:

- 30 friaries
- 28 abbeys
- 26 priories
- 23 nunneries
- 13 cells[1]

Nuns got the boot, too.

1. A monastic cell was a small community of monks or nuns living away from the main monastery, but still under their authority and rule. They often allowed a small group of monks/nuns to live there and oversee the lands.

The Dissolution in Yorkshire year by year

Closed in 1536
Coverham Abbey, Coverham
Haltemprice Priory, Willerby
Sawley Abbey, Sawley

Closed in 1537
Easby Abbey, near Richmond
Jervaulx Abbey, near Ripon

Closed in 1538
Bridlington Priory, Bridlington
Byland Abbey, near Thirsk
Rievaulx Abbey, near Helmsley
Roche Abbey, near Maltby

Closed in 1539
Bolton Abbey, near Harrogate
Fountains Abbey, near Ripon
Kirkstall Abbey, near Leeds
Meaux Abbey, near Beverley
Mount Grace Priory[1], near Northallerton
Selby Abbey, Selby
St Mary's Abbey, York

Closed in 1540
Guisborough Priory, Guisborough
Whitby Abbey, Whitby

1. *The last monastery established in Yorkshire, founded in 1398.*

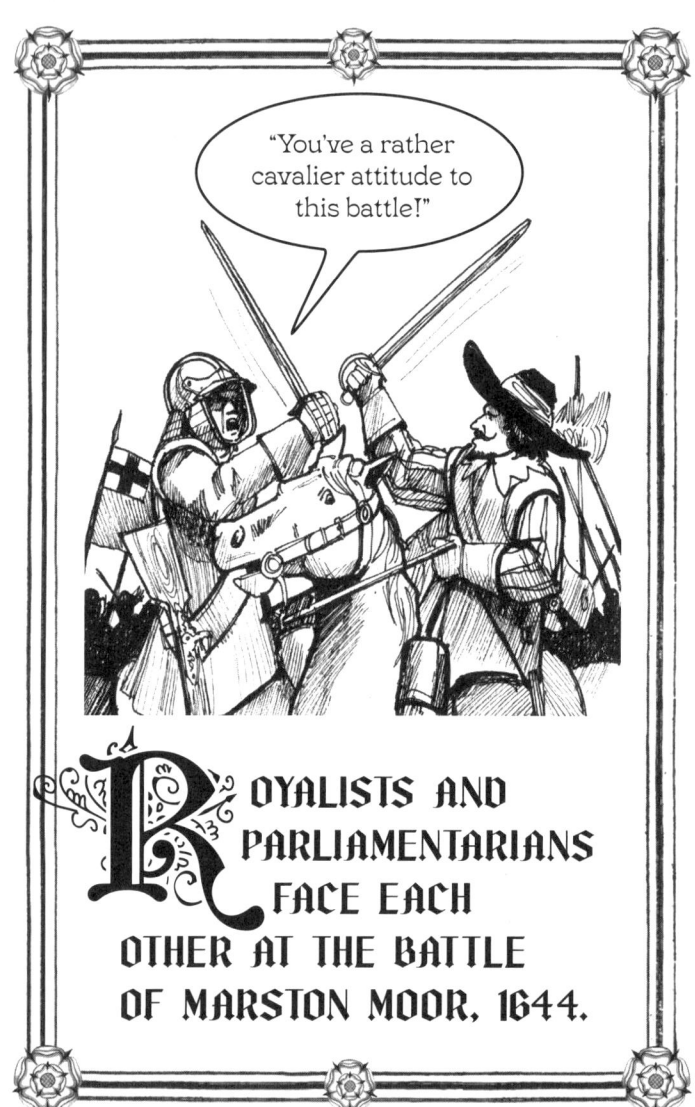

Chapter Ten

Rebels, Royalists & Roundheads

There's no easy way to say this, but the north of England has a long and honourable history of annoying the monarchy and the government.

Given that Yorkshire is a long way from England's traditional power base in the south (in other words, London), how did the likes of Richard III, Henry VIII, Elizabeth I and Charles I keep their beady eyes on the troublesome part of their kingdom up north? The answer they came up with was the Council of the North.

Council of the North

There's nothing like keeping it in the family. The family was the House of York, who provided England with three kings one year:

Yorkist kings of England in 1483

Edward IV
He died in April 1483 and was succeeded by his son, Edward V.

Edward V
A 12-year-old boy, who was king of England for just 78 days before vanishing without trace.

Richard III[1]
The brother of Edward IV and uncle of Edward V, who became king in June 1483. He might have had something to do with young Edward's disappearance, so he could be king instead.

---

[1]. *There were only ever three kings from the House of York, and Richard III was the last of them. He was killed at the Battle of Bosworth in 1485, the last major conflict in the Wars of the Roses, and was the last king of England to die in battle.*

Rebels, Royalists & Roundheads

No sooner had Richard III become king than he set up the King's Council of the North, which was based in Yorkshire. It was a court whose purpose was to maintain law and order in the north – a way for the king to show he was in charge of the north, even though he probably wasn't there in person.

Fast-forward to 1536, by which time Henry VIII was king and the Council had been allowed to lapse. Along comes Robert Aske, the Pilgrimage of Grace and the capture of York (see page 121).

The Council should have been looking after the king's interests in Yorkshire, but it had been caught off-guard by the aforementioned Mr Aske. The northern rebellion went ahead with little to stop it.

This was a huge embarrassment for King Henry, who risked losing a big chunk of northern England to the rebels. So, after Mr Aske had been dealt with, Henry made sure the Council got its act back together.

He made York the permanent base of the Council. It became the king's northern 'eyes and ears'. York became England's second city after London, and

Yorkshire A Very Peculiar History

all because the Council was there. Its headquarters were the former house of the Abbot of St Mary's Abbey, York.[1]

Fast-forward again, this time to 1605, when James I was king (reigned 1603–25). Like King Henry before him, King James also faced a problem in the north or, to be precise, a problem *from* the north.

Gunpowder, treason and plot

One of England's most famous rebels (or heroes, depending on which side you take) was born and raised in York, in 1570.

His name was Guy Fawkes, he went to the town's St Peter's School, and when he was sixteen he became a Catholic, which was a dangerous thing to do at that time.

Thanks to Henry VIII and his children Edward VI and Elizabeth I, Catholics in England were having a hard time practising their faith. This was because:

---

1. *Henry VIII got his hands on this building in 1539, after he closed down St Mary's Abbey. Today, it's known as King's Manor and is part of the University of York.*

Rebels, Royalists & Roundheads

- Henry had broken England away from the Catholic Church (see page 120).
- Henry had set up the English Church with himself as its head, not the Pope.
- Edward made the Catholic Mass illegal.
- Edward ordered the clergy to remove statues of saints from churches, and cover up religious wall paintings.
- Elizabeth became Supreme Governor of the Church of England and Catholics who refused to accept this faced execution.

Guy Fawkes was one of thousands of Catholics who felt that things had gone too far. The final straw came in February 1604, when King James ordered Catholic priests to leave England.

Fawkes teamed up with a group of Catholic men who hatched a plot to blow up the king. The plan was to start an uprising in which Catholics would seize power and return England to being a Catholic nation.

They almost got away with it, but on the night of 4 November 1605, Guy Fawkes was discovered by the king's men. He was hiding in a cellar underneath the Houses of Parliament, London.

Yorkshire A Very Peculiar History

It seemed suspicious, and when bundles of firewood were moved, barrels of gunpowder were found. Fawkes was an explosives expert, and it was his job to set off the bomb he'd been guarding. Instead, he was sent to the gallows.

The government decided that 5 November should become 'a day of thanksgiving'. Known as Bonfire Night or Guy Fawkes Day, it's when effigies of Guy Fawkes – called 'guys' – are burned on bonfires all over Britain. Except, that is, at St Peter's School, York, where a headmaster is reputed to have decreed: "We do not burn effigies of old boys!"

Good riddance to the lot of them!

Guy Fawkes had an explosive character.

York – capital of England

A final fast-forward, to 1641. King Charles I was king (reigned 1625-49), and he was having a few problems, to put it mildly.

In a nutshell, King Charles believed he had a divine right to rule. Charles said he was answerable to no one except God. Parliament started to question this age-old belief, and said *they* should have the power to raise taxes, spend money and dish out punishments, not the king.

St Margaret of York

Margaret Clitherow, a butcher's wife from York, also died for her faith. In 1586 she was arrested in York, charged with giving shelter to Catholic priests.

She was executed on 17 March (Good Friday) 1586. She was made to lie on a sharp stone, a door was placed on her and heavy stones were piled on top until she was crushed to death.

Yorkshire A Very Peculiar History

There was also a question hanging over Charles about his faith. He sympathised with Catholics, and was widely disliked for it.

The scene was set for a fight between the king and his supporters (Royalists or Cavaliers) and parliament (parliamentarians or Roundheads).

Parliament began to take action in 1641, when it shut down the Council of the North. In their view, the Council was a supporter for Catholic Recusants,[1] and was on the king's side.

In April 1642, Charles left London and moved to York with his court. He moved into the King's Manor building (where the Council of the North had been) and for the next six months York was capital of England.

War in our own backyard

1642 was a milestone year for king and country. Across England, troops were mustered and towns declared whether they were Royalist or Parliamentarian.

---

1. *Catholics who refused to give up their Catholic faith and attend Church of England services.*

On 24 April, Charles and a force of Royalists travelled to Hull, a Parliamentarian town. He hoped to take the town and its stockpile of guns, ammunition and explosives. He was refused entry and sent packing. A few weeks later he returned and besieged the town (the First Siege of Hull, July 1642).

The slide into war had begun, and Yorkshire, like many English counties, was divided between supporters of the king and supporters of parliament. The county was the battleground for some of the fiercest fighting of the English Civil War.

The Siege of York, 1644

The Scots invaded northern England on 19 January 1644, and ten days later a Royalist army set off from Yorkshire to stop their advance south. This left Yorkshire vulnerable to attack, which is what happened.

While the Scots were doing a good job of distracting the Royalist army, Parliamentary forces captured Selby, North Yorkshire. From Selby it was only a short march of 24 km

Yorkshire A Very Peculiar History

Battle of Seacroft Moor

Date	30 March 1643
Location	Seacroft, West Yorkshire
Royalists	1,000 cavalry
Parliamentarians	150 cavalry some infantry
Royalists killed	unknown
Parliamentarians killed	200
Result	Royalist victory

The Battle of Seacroft Moor, fought north of Leeds, was more of a major skirmish than a full-blown battle.

Parliamentarian forces were cornered by a much larger Royalist force, who mounted an unstoppable charge aimed at the foot soldiers.

The Parliamentarian cavalry did their best to defend their position, but were outnumbered by the Royalist cavalry almost ten to one. It was a crushing defeat for the Parliamentarians, whose leader, Sir Thomas Fairfax, described it as *"the greatest loss we ever received"*.

Rebels, Royalists & Roundheads

Battle of Adwalton Moor

Date	30 June 1643
Location	Adwalton, West Yorkshire
Royalists	5,000 cavalry 5,000 infantry
Parliamentarians	500 cavalry 3,500 infantry
Royalists killed	unknown
Parliamentarians killed	500
Result	Royalist victory

The Battle of Adwalton Moor was fought on high ground near Bradford.

It was a decisive Royalist victory that reigned most of northern England into the kings control. The whole of Yorkshire – with the exception of Hull, which remained in Parliamentarian hands – had become a Royalist stronghold. But the tide of Royalist success was about to turn.

Parliament signed a treaty with the Scots, who agreed to invade northern England with an army of 20,000 men. By January 1644, the Scottish invasion force was ready.

Yorkshire A Very Peculiar History

(15 miles) north to York – the Royalist's northern headquarters.

The Royalist army returned to Yorkshire, hotly pursued by the Scots, who joined up with their Parliamentarian allies on 20 April at Tadcaster, 16 km (10 miles) west of York.

By early June, York was surrounded by a Parliamentary army of 40,000. A mine (bomb) was set off under St Mary's Tower, which collapsed along with part of the town wall.

The siege ended when King Charles's nephew, Prince Rupert, arrived with 14,500 troops.

Rebels, Royalists & Roundheads

Battle of Marston Moor

Date	2 July 1644
Location	Long Marston, North Yorkshire
Royalists	6,000 cavalry 11,000 infantry
Parliamentarians	7,000 cavalry 15,000 infantry
Royalists killed	4,000
Royalists captured	1,500
Parliamentarians killed	300
Result	Parliamentarian victory

The Parliamentarians and Scots were chased to Marston Moor, 10 km (6 miles) west of York. In the battle that followed, the Royalists suffered a crushing defeat from which they never recovered.

The Siege of York was renewed, and the city surrendered on 15 July 1644. After that, Parliamentarian forces took Royalist castles across the county, and by the end of 1645 Yorkshire's part in the Civil War was over.

Ten Things You Didn't Know About the Civil War in Yorkshire

1. Scarborough, North Yorkshire, changed hands seven times between 1642 and 1648, with two long sieges in 1645 and 1648.

2. When Royalist troops attacked Bradford, West Yorkshire, on 18 December 1642, the town's citizens held them off. A Royalist officer was struck down, and pleaded for 'quarter' (mercy). Not knowing what the word meant, a local man, Ralph Atkinson, shouted that he would give him 'Bradford Quarter' and killed him. It became a soldiers' term for 'no mercy'.

3. Leeds, West Yorkshire, was captured by Parliamentarian forces in January 1643. Some of the defending Royalists drowned as they tried to swim across the River Aire.

4. The taking of Selby, North Yorkshire, in 1644 was a major success for the Parliamentarians. They captured 80 Royalist officers, 1,600 soldiers, 4 cannon, 2,000 muskets and other guns, 7 barrels of gunpowder and a large quantity of ammunition. The weapons were put to use by the Parliamentarians.

5. At the start of the Siege of York, the Royalist defenders tried to burn down buildings outside Bootham Bar, but the Parliamentarians captured the fire-raisers.

6. The Parliamentarians put two mines under the walls of York, but only one exploded. The other bomb failed to go off because the chamber it was in filled up with water.

7. The Battle of Marston Moor began at about seven o'clock in the evening, and lasted for about two hours.

8. A condition of the surrender of York was that the city would be occupied only by Yorkshiremen, which is what happened. They respected their 'mother city', and although many buildings were destroyed, the city's magnificent churches were not looted by the Parliamentarian troops.

9. Skipton Castle, North Yorkshire, was the last Royalist stronghold in Yorkshire. It surrendered to the Parliamentarians on 21 December 1645, and then the whole of Yorkshire was under their control.

10. And finally ... at the trial of King Charles I in 1649, fifteen Yorkshiremen were among the judges, and six were present at his execution, showing Yorkshire's significant contribution to one of the most transformative periods in English history.

Chapter Eleven

Made in Yorkshire and proud of it!

When the dust eventually settled after the bitter Civil War of the 1640s, peace finally returned to Yorkshire. However, an even bigger conflict loomed around the corner – the 'battle' between town and country. Over the course of the next two hundred years, Yorkshire changed from an agricultural county to an industrial one. Farmers moved off the land and into the growing towns and factories in search of work and new lifestyles. Britain was entering the industrial age, and Yorkshire was never the same again.

Yorkshire A Very Peculiar History

The population boom

In the 1670s, Yorkshire's population was between 350,000 and 430,000, and of these, half lived in the West Riding of Yorkshire.[1] The county town, York, had a population of around 12,000, and Leeds, the second largest-town, about 6,000.

In 1801, when the first census[2] was taken of the population of England and Wales, 859,133 people were recorded as living in Yorkshire. In a little over a century, the county's population had doubled.

It then took only fifty years to double again, so that by 1851 there were 1,797,995 people in the whole of Yorkshire. The West Riding still claimed the lion's share of the population, but now it had three out of every four Yorkshirefolk living in and around its thriving towns of Leeds, Bradford and Sheffield.

---

1. The West Riding of Yorkshire was roughly the area covered by present-day West Yorkshire, South Yorkshire and parts of North Yorkshire, Lancashire, Cumbria and Greater Manchester. It was abolished in 1974 (see page 13).

2. A census is when the government counts all the people living in a country to learn about them, like how many there are and where they live.

— Made in Yorkshire and proud of it! —

Yorkshire's population grew rapidly throughout the century, and by 1901 the county's population stood at 3,489,559.

This was the period of the Industrial Revolution, when Britain was the 'workshop of the world', and when the industries of Yorkshire were second to none.

Where they lived in 1851

The census of 1851 found that Yorkshire had twelve towns with more than 10,000 inhabitants. Nine of the towns were in the West Riding.

Town	Population	Riding
Leeds	101,343	West
Sheffield	83,447	West
Bradford	52,493	West
Hull	50,670	East
York	36,622	East
Huddersfield	30,880	West
Scarborough	25,830	North
Halifax	25,159	West
Wakefield	16,929	West
Barnsley	14,913	West
Dewsbury	14,049	West
Doncaster	12,052	West

Yorkshire A Very Peculiar History

The textile industry

Of Yorkshire's industries, the textile industry (wool, worsted[1] and, to a lesser extent, cotton and silk) has always been the most important.

The Yorkshire countryside is ideally suited to sheep farming, with a plentiful supply of pasture for sheep to graze. In the Middle Ages, the county's monks kept huge flocks of sheep, whose wool they sold to merchants.

Smaller flocks were kept by individual farmers. Many farmers processed the fleeces themselves, weaving woollen yarn into cloth on handlooms. They took the finished cloth, known as a 'piece' (a 27m / 30-yard length), to a nearby town for sale at a 'piece hall'. Halifax Piece Hall, which opened in 1779, was one of Yorkshire's largest, with 300 separate rooms set around a courtyard.

---

1. *Woollen cloth made from best-quality yarn. It has a smoother, less whiskery texture than other types of woollen cloth. It's named after the Norfolk village of Worstead, where the cloth was produced in the Middle Ages, long before it was made in the West Riding.*

A handweaver's life

Cornelius Ashworth (1752-1821) was a farmer and handloom weaver from Ovenden, near Halifax. He wrote a diary in which he recorded his daily work, the weather (very important for farmers then, as now), and events he'd been to. Here are some of his entries:

1 November 1782 *A fine frosty clear drafty day. Sized a warp [soaked woollen threads] and churned [made butter] in the forenoon. Wove 5 yards.*

4 November 1782 *Wove 6 ¾ yards.*

2 July 1783 *A dull day very hot with a good deal of thunder and a little rain in the afternoon. I carried my piece to Halifax. In the afternoon weeded garden and other jobs.*

16 August 1783 *I churned, sized a warp in the morning. Went to Halifax and saw two men hanged on Becon Hill, sentenced at York for activity in riot.*

11 July 1784 *Employed in filling up the part of the dam and other work. Went to Halifax and bought a new hat at twelve shillings. Had a new wheelbarrow brought home.*

Yorkshire A Very Peculiar History

For centuries, farmer-weavers like Cornelius Ashworth had woven woollen cloth at home on handlooms. It was a cottage industry, and it was wiped out by the factory system.

In the 1770s, factories powered by water had started to transform the cotton industry in Lancashire. By the 1790s, steam power was replacing water power.

The factory system spread into the West Riding of Yorkshire from neighbouring Lancashire, and the county's first textile factories were built at Keighley and Addingham in the 1790s. They sped up the process of spinning cotton.

After Yorkshire's cotton industry, it was the county's worsted industry that took up the new technology of the industrial age, but the woollen industry lagged behind.

Although mills with machines for spinning wool into yarn were built in the 1820s, the age-old practice of weaving it into cloth by hand carried on for many years.

Trouble at t'mill

The factory system wasn't to everyone's liking because machines were doing people out of their jobs. In 1812, mills and machines in Leeds and Huddersfield were damaged by men who feared losing their jobs. They were known as Luddites.

William Horsfall, the owner of a mill at Ottiwells, near Huddersfield, was shot and killed by George Mellor. Mellor was arrested, and together with sixteen fellow Luddites was hanged at York. Seven others were transported to Australia.

The pace of industrial change was remarkable. In just five years, between 1833 and 1838, the number of West Riding mills jumped from 129 to 606 - a rate of 95 new mills being opened each year. By 1850, the area had 880 mills. Ultimately there were nearly 2,000 mills in the West Riding.

One of the most famous mills was Salt's Mill, near Bradford. It was built in the 1850s by Titus Salt (1803-76), who even built a village for the mill's workers to live in. The village was named Saltaire – a combination of the founder's surname with the name of the local river, the River Aire.

Saltaire was a great improvement on the slum housing many of the workers were used to. It had wash houses with running water, a hospital, library, concert hall, billiard room, gymnasium and a school.

Yorkshire slavery

Richard Oastler (1789-1861), a factory reformer from Leeds, was shocked that children worked in Yorkshire's mills. He wrote a letter to the Leeds Mercury (16 October 1830) describing them as places of slavery. Here's part of his letter:

"Thousands of little children, both male and female, but principally female, from seven to fourteen years of age, are daily compelled to labour from six o'clock in the morning to seven in the evening, with only - Britons, blush while you read it! - with only thirty minutes allowed for eating and recreation."

Five Things You Didn't Know About Yorkshire's Textile Industry

1. Lister's Mill, Bradford, built in 1871, was the largest silk factory in the world. During the Second World War, it produced 2,140 km (1,330 miles) of parachute silk.

2. In 1813, Benjamin Law invented shoddy – a type of soft woollen cloth made from shredded rags, old woollen goods and waste from spinning and weaving. It was mainly made in the mills of Dewsbury, Ossett and Batley. Today, 'shoddy' has come to mean anything that is poor quality.

3. Mungo was invented at a similar time as shoddy. A tougher cloth, also made from waste products, it was used for army greatcoats. Its name might come from the Yorkshire word for a mongrel dog – a mungo. Like the dog, the cloth was also the result of a mixture.

4. By 1850, the West Riding produced 90 per cent of all Britain's worsted goods.

5. Today, cloth woven by A. W. Hainsworth & Sons at Pudsey, West Yorkshire, is supplied to the British Army for parade uniforms. They also make the smoothest, fastest snooker cloth in the world!

The steel industry

Yorkshire's steel industry was centred on the south of the county, and one town more than any other: Sheffield. Steel was first made in the Sheffield area in the 1640s, and as the raw materials of the industry – coal and iron ore – were in plentiful supply nearby, many forges and furnaces were set up.

By the 1740s, Sheffield was becoming known for the manufacture of steel cutlery – and then a Sheffield steel-maker invented a new type of steel that eventually made Sheffield world famous.

He was Benjamin Huntsman (1704-76), a clockmaker from Doncaster. He thought the steel he used for his clock springs wasn't good enough. Huntsman was sure it could be improved, so he began experimenting to find a way of making a harder type of steel. He succeeded, and by 1751 Huntsman was working in Sheffield as a steel-maker.

Made in Yorkshire and proud of it!

Huntsman's invention could have made him a fortune. Instead, his secret method of making cast steel was stolen by a rival who, according to a story, pretended to be a homeless beggar in need of somewhere to sleep.

Helpful Huntsman took pity on the fake beggar and, believing his story, invited him into his workshop where he discovered the inventor's secret.

It's impossible to say if the beggar story is true or not, but the fact is that Huntsman's method of cast-steel production was eventually copied by Sheffield's steel-makers, and the town was on its way to earning its nickname: Steel City.

By 1820, Sheffield was known nationally and internationally for its steel, and for its cutlery. By the 1850s, Sheffield and the surrounding area made 90 per cent of all the steel in Britain.

The coal industry

Coal was the fuel of the Industrial Revolution, and the colliers of Yorkshire went deep beneath the county to dig for this 'black gold'.

The Yorkshire coalfield, covering a large chunk of South Yorkshire from Leeds and Bradford down to Sheffield and Rotherham, became one of Britain's major producers. In 1851, together with the Midland coalfield which it joined on to, some eight million tons of coal was mined.

By the 1860s, there were almost 400 pits working the Yorkshire coalfield, each with its own name. Who knows what was going through the minds of Mr Crawshaw and Mr Blackeley when they named their Dewsbury pit 'Babes in the Wood'! As for the Balaklava pit at Leeds, it was named after the Battle of Balaclava, fought in the Crimea, Russia, in 1854. Pits in the Barnsley area took the name Main, such as Blacker Main, Denaby Main and Edmund's Main. Halifax had

Made in Yorkshire and proud of it!

pits called Bottom – Bank Bottom, Binns Bottom and Harp Bottom.

In 1913, Yorkshire's pits produced 27 million tons of coal – 10 per cent of all the coal mined in Britain that year (this was the peak year for coal production in Britain). In 1929, Yorkshire supplied 33.5 million tons of coal – 13 per cent of all the coal mined in Britain.

Coal – the 'black gold' of Yorkshire

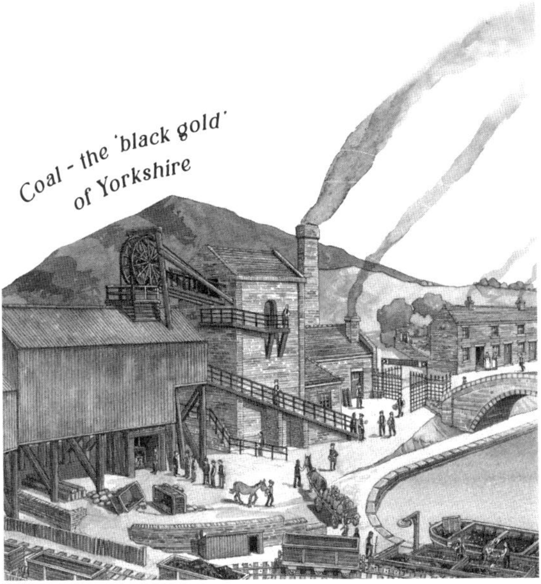

Yorkshire pit disasters

Yorkshire's coal mines were dangerous places where many tragic accidents and disasters occurred.

Huskar Pit, Silkstone, 1838
The pit flooded and many children drowned (James Burkinshaw, 7, Sarah Jukes, 8, Catherine Garnet, 8, and 23 others). This disaster led to the banning of female and child labour underground.

Warren Vale, Rawmarsh, 1851
An explosion killed 52 miners.

Lower Elsecar, Barnsley, 1852
An explosion killed 12 miners. In response, the first underground fan was fitted to improve ventilation and stop dangerous gases from building up.

Lundhill, Barnsley, 1857
An explosion killed 189 men and boys. The Kellett family lost seven sons.

The Oaks, Barnsley, 1866
An explosion killed 361 men and boys. A second explosion killed 27 more, sent down in a rescue party. This was the worst colliery disaster in England, and the second worst in Britain after the Welsh Senghenydd colliery disaster.

Yorkshire pits of the past

In 1984, Yorkshire had 56 working collieries, but when, due to profitability, Cortonwood colliery was threatened with closure, the county's mineworkers (and others across Britain) went on a long and bitter strike. The miners lost, and the government got on with the painful business of shutting down the pits.

Here are some of the many Yorkshire pits that closed over the years.

Pit	Town	Closed
Elsecar Main	Barnsley	1983
Acton Hall	Wakefield	1985
Brookhouse	Rotherham	1985
Cortonwood	Barnsley	1985
Yorkshire Main	Doncaster	1985
Woolley	Wakefield	1987
Barnsley Main	Barnsley	1991
Dinnington	Rotherham	1991
Thurcroft	Rotherham	1991
Grimethorpe	Barnsley	1992
North Selby	Selby	1999
Stillingfleet	Selby	2004
Rossington	Doncaster	2006

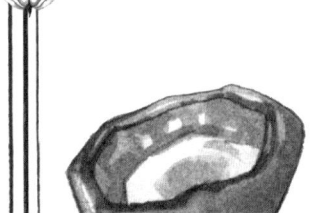

FACT: One company in Hull produces around 20 million frozen Yorkshire puddings a week.

FACT:
In 1998, a racing pigeon was given away by his Skipton owner to a friend in Spain. In 2008, the pigeon flew back to its old loft in Skipton. The bird's name was Boomerang!

Coo! Coo!

FACT: Black pudding, pig's pudding, blood pudding – it's a sausage eaten at breakfast.

Chapter Twelve

Yorkshire Factfile

Did you know that there are more chickens in Yorkshire than people? Or that there are more people than sheep? That in Yorkshire they put custard on their Christmas tusky, and gravy on their pudding? It's a county of surprises, a county of firsts, and a county to explore as you read on with this factfile...

Summat ter eyt or sup?[1]

At the start of a meal, Yorkshirefolk might be heard saying their very own grace:

> *God bless us all,*
> *An' mak us able,*
> *Ta eyt all t' stuff 'at's on this table.*

A Yorkshire Sunday roast dinner (the meal between breakfast and tea) wouldn't be complete without Yorkshire pudding. Made from eggs, flour, milk, water and a little salt and pepper, the ingredients are blended into a batter which is then cooked in a baking tin. Traditionally, the tin was placed under a joint of beef as it roasted. The meat's juices dripped into the pudding mix and were absorbed by it.

Authentic Yorkshire pudding is served *before* the main course, not *with it*. It should be served with beef or onion gravy.

1. *Something to eat or drink?*

Yorkshire Factfile

Christmas tusky

An area between Wakefield, Morley and Rothwell is known as the Rhubarb Triangle. Farmers here produce forced rhubarb (known as tusky), made to grow out of season and be ready at Christmas.

Here are some of Yorkshire's other claims to food fame:

Black pudding
Thick black sausages made from pigs' blood.

Cheese
Yorkshire has several traditional cheeses including Swaledale, Wensleydale, Cotherstone and Coverdale.

Turkey
Britain's first turkeys came to Boynton, near Bridlington, from North America in the 1550s.

Fat rascals
Small, round cakes, similar to scones.

Fish and chips
Britain's national dish was 'reinvented' in the 1920s by Yorkshireman Harry Ramsden.

The Cawood Feast

On 15 January 1464, George Neville held a feast for 2,500 guests at Cawood Castle, near Selby, North Yorkshire, in celebration of becoming Archbishop of York. It became known as the Great Feast of Cawood due to its belly-bursting size. On the menu were:

Meat and fish
- 4,000 pigeons • 4,000 rabbits
- 4,000 pasties and cold venison
- 2,000 geese • 2,000 chickens
- 1,000 sheep • 1,000 capons (cockerels)
- 608 pikes and breams (freshwater fish)
- 500 stags, bucks and roes
- 500 partridges
- 400 mallards and teals (ducks)
- 400 woodcocks (wild birds)
- 400 plovers (wild birds)
- 304 pigs • 304 veals (calves)
- 200 pheasants • 104 oxen
- 104 peacocks • 12 porpoises and seals
- 6 wild bulls

Dessert
- 4,000 cold tarts • 3,000 cold custards
- 2,000 hot custards • 1,000 jellies

Drinks
- 300 casks of ale • 100 casks of wine

Yorkshire Factfile

Claims to fame

Yorkshire has its fair share of quirky characters.

Oldest Briton
Henry Jenkins, buried in Bolton-on-Swale, near Catterick, North Yorkshire, is said to have been 169 years old when he died in 1670.

The Yorkshire Giant
Henry Alexander Cooper (known as Harry), an iron-ore miner from South Skelton, East Yorkshire, was 8ft, 7.75in (2.63m) tall. He ended up in a circus, and died in 1899.

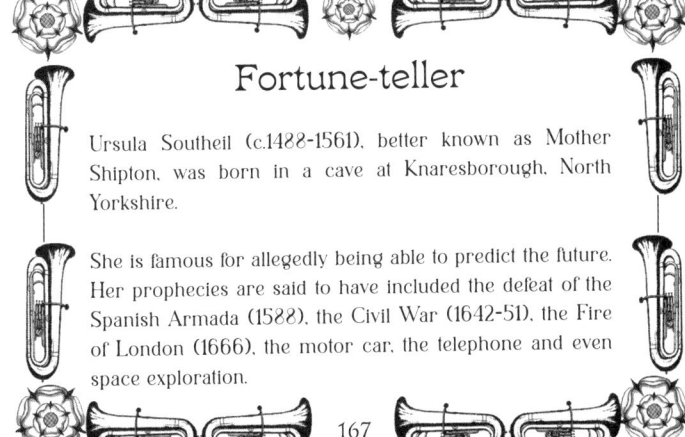

Fortune-teller

Ursula Southeil (c.1488-1561), better known as Mother Shipton, was born in a cave at Knaresborough, North Yorkshire.

She is famous for allegedly being able to predict the future. Her prophecies are said to have included the defeat of the Spanish Armada (1588), the Civil War (1642-51), the Fire of London (1666), the motor car, the telephone and even space exploration.

Yorkshire inventors

From a 'flat-pack' bridge designed to move troops across rivers, to the Little Nipper mousetrap. From a road stud that reflects the light of car headlights, to steel that never rusts – Yorkshire has given them to the world.

Who	What	When
John Harrison	Marine clocks	1700s
George Dunhill	Liquorice sweets	1760
Joseph Bramah	Ballcock	1778
Joseph Hansom	Hansom cab	1834
John Kilner	Glass jars	1842
George Cayley	Glider	1853
James Atkinson	Mousetrap	1897
Percy Shaw	Road cat'seyes	1934
Donald Bailey	Portable bridge	1942

Stainless steel

In 1913, Harry Brearley (1871-1948) invented 'rustless steel' while working at the Brown-Firth Research Laboratory in Sheffield. It became known as 'stainless steel' because it did not rust or tarnish.

Famous sons and daughters

James Cook (1728-79)
Sea captain, born in Marton.

William Wilberforce (1759-1833)
Anti-slavery campaigner, born in Hull.

Frederick Delius (1862-1934)
Composer, born in Bradford.

Henry Moore (1898-1986)
Sculptor, born in Castleford.

Amy Johnson (1903-41)
Pioneer flier, born in Hull.

Leonard Hutton (1916-90)
Ashes-winning cricket captain, born in Pudsey.

Alan Bennett (born 1934)
Playwright and actor, born in Leeds.

Judi Dench (born 1934)
Actress, born in York.

David Hockney (born 1937)
Artist, born in Bradford.

Sean Bean (born 1959)
Actor known for his roles in "The Lord of the Rings" and "Game of Thrones," born in Sheffield.

Jeremy Clarkson (born 1960)
Television presenter and journalist, born in Doncaster.

Helen Sharman (born 1963)
First British astronaut, born in Sheffield.

Jarvis Cocker (born 1963)
Lead singer of the band Pulp, born in Sheffield.

Jessica Ennis-Hill (born 1986)
Olympic gold medalist heptathlete, born in Sheffield.

The Brontë sisters

In the 1800s, three sisters, who lived at Haworth, near Bradford, wrote some of the most famous books in the English language:

- Anne Brontë wrote *Agnes Grey*.
- Emily Brontë wrote *Wuthering Heights*.
- Charlotte Brontë wrote *Jane Eyre*.

On the farm

Every year, the Department for Environment, Food and Rural Affairs counts the animals on Britain's farms. In 2009, Yorkshire had:

Animal	Total
Chickens	13,057,261
Sheep	2,116,969
Pigs	1,255,562
Cattle	568,343
Ducks	538,612
Turkeys	399,061
Horses	26,662
Goats	14,424
Geese	11,551

Where to see sea birds

Britain's largest gathering of sea birds is at Bempton Cliffs, East Yorkshire. Between April and August the cliffs are home to 200,000 noisy gannets, fulmars, guillemots, razorbills, kittiwakes and puffins.

Fur and feather

Sheep on the moors, birds on the cliffs, and man's best friend – they're all in Yorkshire.

Swaledale sheep
A hardy breed with off-white wool and curled horns. Able to live on the Yorkshire uplands in all weathers. A symbol of the Yorkshire Dales.

Yorkshire Terrier and Airedale Terrier
The little dog known as a Yorkie was developed in the 1800s by coal miners. The Airedale came from Barnsley in the 1860s.

Whippet
A long dog, like a greyhound but smaller, once used by Yorkshire coal miners for racing.

Ferret-legging
Ferret-legging was popular among coal miners in Yorkshire, who competed to see who could keep a wriggling ferret down their trousers the longest. For 29 years, the world record was 5 hrs 26 mins, set by Reg Mellor. It was beaten in 2010 by a retired headmaster from Staffordshire.

Cricket

Cricket has been played in Yorkshire since at least 1751. Sheffield Cricket Club, which began around this time, is the ancestor of Yorkshire County Cricket Club. Some of YCCC's records are:

County titles won
31 including 1 shared (most by any club)

Highest score
887 against Warwickshire (1896)

Most runs in a career
38,561 by Herbert Sutcliffe (1919-45)

Most runs in one season
2,883 by Herbert Sutcliffe (1932)

Most wickets
3,608 by Wilfred Rhodes (1898-1930)

FACT: From 1863 to 1992, YCCC was famous for insisting that its players must have been born in Yorkshire. The rule was dropped in 1992.

Rugby

Yorkshire is the birthplace of rugby league. It came about in 1895, when twenty-two Yorkshire, Lancashire and Cheshire clubs broke away from the Rugby Union and set up the Northern Rugby Football Union. They agreed to do this at a meeting held in Huddersfield. In 1922, the NRFU changed its name to the Rugby Football League.

Yorkshire clubs who formed the Northern Union in 1895

- Batley FC
- Bradford FC
- Brighouse Rovers FC
- Broughton Rangers FC
- Halifax FC
- Huddersfield FC
- Hull FC
- Hunslet FC
- Leeds FC
- Liversedge FC
- Manningham FC
- Wakefield Trinity FC

FACT: The biggest attendance at a rugby league game was in 1954, when 102,569 supporters squeezed into Odsal Stadium, Bradford, to watch Halifax vs. Warrington.

Football

Yorkshire's place in footballing history starts with Sheffield Football Club[1]. It is the world's oldest football club, founded in 1857, and began life when players from the town's cricket club started playing football after their cricket season had ended for the year.

Two of the Sheffield FC players (Nathaniel Creswick and William Prest) devised a set of rules for the new club, known as the Sheffield Rules. As more clubs were formed in the Sheffield area, they agreed to follow the same rules. These rules became the basis of the Football Association's rules (the Laws of the Game) when they were created in 1863.

What Sheffield Rules have given to football:

- Free kicks for fouls
- Corners
- Throw-ins

---

1. *Not to be confused with Sheffield Wednesday Football Club (founded in 1867) or Sheffield United Football Club (founded in 1889).*

Yorkshire dictionary

Yorkshire	Definition
allus	always
aye	yes
babby	baby
baggin	packed lunch
cack-'anded	left-handed, clumsy
chuffed	pleased, excited
dale	valley
dursn't	dare not
ee by gum!	oh, my word!
ey up!	look out!
fantickles	freckles
fatther	father
gander	look at
gerr away!	get away!
hast ta?	have you?
hutch up	move over
in't	in the
jiggered	very tired
kecks	trousers or underwear
lass	girl
lewk	look
manky	not nice, rotten
mardy	moody, sulky
nouse	sense
nowt	nothing
'ow do?	how are you? hello
owt	anything
parkin	type of gingerbread

parky	chilly
reet	right
rift	to burp
scran	food
sithee	I'll see thee
thissen	yourself
thosty	thirsty
uggrum	pig
urchin	hedgehog
wang	throw
watter	water
yam	home
yed	head

Some Yorkshire sayings

- 'Put t'wood in t'oil': Put the wood in the hole (close the door).

- 'Sit thissen dahn an' tell me abaht it': Sit yourself down and tell me about it.

- 'Tha' can allus tell a Yorkshireman, but tha' can't tell 'im much": You can always tell a Yorkshireman, but you can't tell him much.

Highest, longest, deepest

Highest mountain: Mickle Fell, 788m (2,585ft) North Pennines, and just within the historic county of Yorkshire.

Largest natural lake: Hornsea Mere, west of Hornsea, East Yorkshire, 189 hectares (467 acres).

Highest waterfall above ground: Hardraw Force, Yorkshire Dales, 30m (100ft).

Highest waterfall below ground: Inside Gaping Gill cave system, North Yorkshire, 102m (335ft).

Highest earth-filled dam: Scammonden, near Huddersfield, West Yorkshire, 73.76m (242ft).

Highest sea-cliff: Boulby, North Yorkshire, 203m (666ft).

Deepest well: In St James's Square, Boroughbridge, North Yorkshire, 78m (256ft).

Longest river: River Aire, 142km (88 miles).

Longest place name in England: Sutton-under-Whitestonecliffe, North Yorkshire (27 letters).

Largest natural underground chamber: Gaping Gill, North Yorkshire, 140m long, 27m wide, 34m high (460ft by 89ft by 112ft).

Deepest cave: Gaping Gill, North Yorkshire, 197.5m (648ft) deep.

Tallest tree: A lime tree at Duncombe Park near Helmsley, North Yorkshire, 47m (154ft).

Longest station seat in Europe: A wooden bench at Scarborough Station is 139m (456ft) long. It seats 228 passengers.

Longest, deepest and highest canal tunnel: Standedge Tunnel, West Yorkshire, on the Huddersfield Narrow Canal. It is 5,029m (16,499 ft) long, 194m (636ft) underground at the deepest point, and 196 m (643ft) above sea level.

Yorkshire Day

The shake-up to the historic county of Yorkshire in 1974, which did away with the Ridings and brought in the new counties of North, West and South Yorkshire (see page 13), did something else as well.

The following year, the Yorkshire Ridings Society created Yorkshire Day – a day to celebrate the historic county of Yorkshire. The date chosen was 1 August.

Acknowledgements

In writing this book, I have relied on the valuable work of others. In particular, the following books have been essential reading, and I recommend them to anyone who wishes to know more about the county of Yorkshire:

A History of Yorkshire: County of the Broad Acres, David Hey (Carnegie Publishing, 2005)

A Yorkshire Miscellany, Tom Holman (Frances Lincoln, 2008)

The Yorkshire Dictionary of Dialect, Tradition and Folklore, Arnold Kellett (Smith Settle, second edition, 2002)

Battlefield Yorkshire: From the Romans to the English Civil Wars, David Cooke (Pen & Sword, 2006)

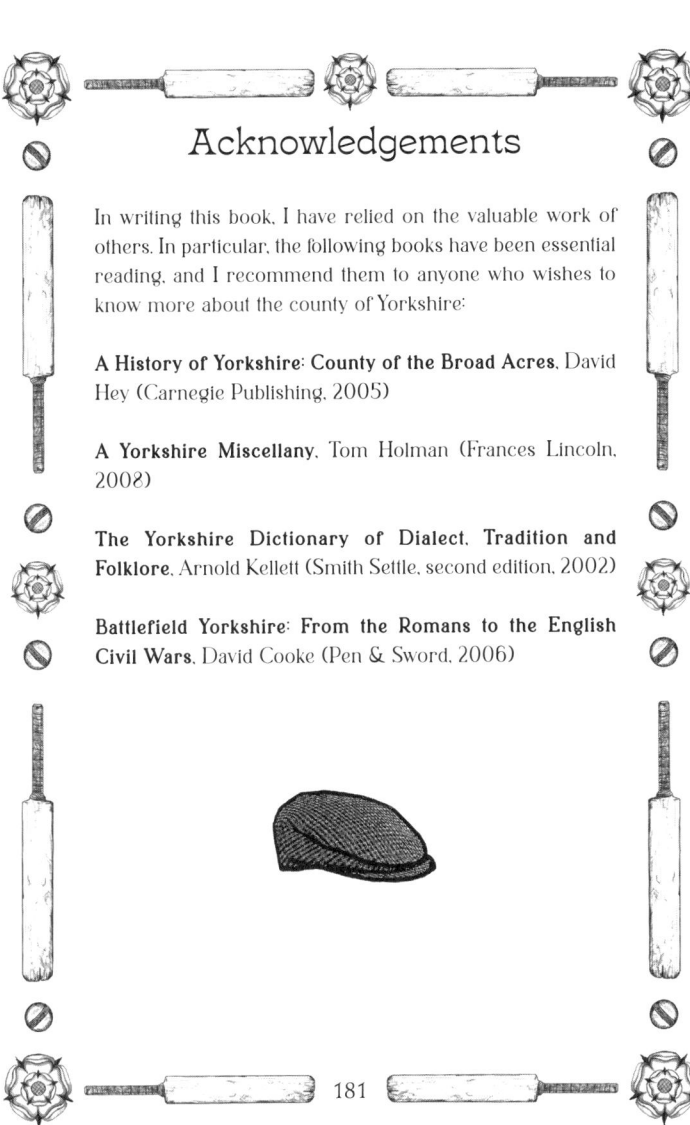

Yorkshire A Very Peculiar History

Glossary

abbot The head person of a monastery.

amber Fossilised resin from ancient trees, usually found washed up on beaches.

bailey An area at the foot of a motte where buildings stood. It was surrounded by a rampart.

barrow A prehistoric burial mound.

Brigantes An Iron Age British tribe whose homeland was centred on Yorkshire.

cloister A covered walkway in a monastery, open along one side.

cottage industry When something is made on a small-scale, often from a person's home.

handloom A machine used to weave cloth, operated by hand.

Luddite A person who destroyed factory machines because they were causing workers to lose their jobs. Named after Ned Ludd, a weaver from Leicestershire.

minster An early church built as a missionary teaching church, from where Christianity could spread.

monastery The place where a community of monks live, often built in a secluded, quiet place.

moneyer A person whose job was to produce coins.

motte A mound of soil on which a small timber castle was built.

mungo A type of tough woollen cloth made from waste or old wool.

Parliamentarian A soldier in the English Civil War who supported Parliament. Also known as a Roundhead.

pestilence An epidemic disease; plague.

Glossary

pewter A soft grey metal made from tin and lead, used for kitchen utensils and tableware.

piece A length of woven woollen cloth.

rampart An embankment of earth built around a fort or a castle; a defensive structure.

refectory The dining area of a monastery.

Riding Yorkshire used to be divided into three parts called Ridings, from an Old English word meaning 'thirds'.

Royalist A soldier in the English Civil War who supported the king. Also known as a Cavalier.

shoddy A type of soft woollen cloth made from waste or old wool.

slum A very poor type of house.

transported A punishment once used in Britain in which people were sent (transported) to lands overseas, such as Australia.

tusky Rhubarb.

tyke A nickname for a person from Yorkshire.

worsted A type of smooth woollen cloth made from best-quality yarn.

yarn Fine thread used for weaving.

Yorkshire A Very Peculiar History

Timeline of Yorkshire history

c.9,000 BC	The oldest-known evidence of human activity in Yorkshire, from Victoria Cave, near Settle.
c.8,700 BC	Mesolithic hunter-gatherers set up Star Carr camp at the edge of Lake Pickering, near Scarborough.
c.3,500 BC	Three Neolithic henges built at Thornborough, near Ripon.
c.1,800 BC	The Ferriby Bronze Age boat was made.
c.1,600 BC	The Rudston Monolith, a standing stone, was set up.
c.500s BC	Yorkshire becomes the homeland of the Brigantes tribe.
c.300 BC	An Iron Age log boat found at Hasholme was made.
AD 50s–60s	Reign of Queen Cartimandua, last ruler of the Brigantes.
68/69	King Venutius tries to overthrow Queen Cartimandua.
71	Eboracum (York) is founded by the Roman Ninth Legion. Becomes military capital of northern Britain.
70s	Romans defeat the Brigantes, somewhere near Scotch Corner.
80s	Yorkshire is pacified and becomes part of Roman Britain.
100s	Roman fort at York rebuilt in stone; pottery industry established at Cantley, near Doncaster.
122	Emperor Hadrian visits York.
211	Emperor Severus dies in York.

Timeline of Yorkshire history

214	York becomes the capital of Britannia Inferior (Lower Britain).
293	York becomes the capital of Britannia Secunda (Lesser Britain).
300s	Roman York declines.
306	Emperor Constantius I dies in York.
306	Constantine is declared emperor in York.
450s	Start of the Anglian kingdom of Deira, East Yorkshire.
c.600	Battle of Catterick, between Britons and Angles.
600s	Kingdom of Deira covers all Yorkshire, with Eoforwic (York) as its capital. Joins with Anglian kingdom of Bernicia to form the Anglo-Saxon kingdom of Northumbria. York is capital of Northumbria.
627	King Edwin of Northumbria is baptised in York.
633	Battle of Hatfield Chase, near Doncaster, between Northumbrians and Mercians. King Edwin is killed.
655	Battle of Winwidfield, near Leeds, between Northumbrians and Mercians. Mercian King Penda is killed.
866	Vikings capture York, which they name Jorvik.
876	Halfdan becomes the first Viking king of Jorvik.
927	Athelstan, Anglo-Saxon king of Wessex, seizes Jorvik from the Vikings.
937	Battle of Brunanburgh, possibly in the Rotherham/Sheffield area, between Anglo-Saxons and Vikings and their British allies.

Yorkshire A Very Peculiar History

954	Battle of Stainmore. Eric Bloodaxe, the last Viking king of York, is killed. Yorkshire is absorbed into the emerging kingdom of England.
1065	First recorded use of the name 'Yorkshire'.
1066	Battle of Fulford Bridge, near York, between Vikings and English. York is captured by Vikings. Battle of Stamford Bridge, near York, between Vikings and English. Viking king is killed.
1068	Norman King William I (the Conqueror) arrives in York. A motte-and-bailey castle is built.
	York's second motte-and-bailey castle is built
1069	Yorkshire's first monastery, Selby Abbey, is founded.
1069–70	The Harrying of the North, in which much of northern England was laid to waste by the Normans.
1138	Battle of the Standard, Northallerton. A Norman army defeats a Scottish army.
1190	Massacre of Jews at York Castle.
1220s	Work begins on building York Minster.
1328	King Edward III marries Philippa of Hainault in York Minster.
1349	Black Death plague reaches Yorkshire.
1400	King Richard II dies at Pontefract Castle.
1455	Wars of the Roses begin.
1460	Battle of Wakefield, West Yorkshire; Richard, Duke of York, is killed.
1461	Battle of Towton, North Yorkshire; Edward, Duke of York, crowned King Edward IV.

Timeline of Yorkshire history

1483	Council of the North established in York.
1536	Dissolution of the Monasteries begins; Pilgrimage of Grace; rebels seize York.
1568	Mary, Queen of Scots, is imprisoned at Bolton Castle.
1570	Guy Fawkes born in York.
1586	Margaret Clitherow executed in York.
1641	Council of the North closed down.
1642	King Charles I makes York his capital; First Siege of Hull in the English Civil War.
1643	Battles of Seacroft Moor and Adwalton Moor, West Yorkshire.
1644	Siege of York; Battle of Marston Moor, North Yorkshire.
1645	Surrender of Skipton Castle to Parliamentarians.
1740s	Rise of the Sheffield cutlery industry.
1779	Halifax Piece Hall built.
1790s	Factory system comes to Yorkshire, with cotton mills built at Keighley and Addingham.
1812	Textile machines damaged in Huddersfield by Luddites.
1850s	Salt's Mill built at Saltaire, near Bradford; Sheffield produces 90 per cent of all Britain's steel.
1860s	400 collieries working in Yorkshire.
1895	Rugby league established at a meeting in Huddersfield.
1913	Stainless steel invented in Sheffield.
1929	Yorkshire collieries produce 13 per cent of all coal mined in Britain.
1942	York is bombed by the German Luftwaffe.

Yorkshire A Very Peculiar History

1974	Local government reorganisation abolishes the Yorkshire Ridings and replaces them with new counties.
1976–81	The Coppergate Viking dig, in York.
1984	York Minster damaged by fire; Jorvik Viking Centre opens, in York.
2007	Vale of York Viking Hoard discovered.
1976–81	The Coppergate Viking dig in York.
1984	York Minster damaged by fire; Jorvik Viking Centre opens, in York.
2007	Vale of York Viking Hoard discovered.
2020	The Ryedale Hoard is discovered by metal dectorists and contains some of Yorkshire's most significant Roman objects, including an 1,800 year old bust of the Roman Emperor Marcus Aurelius.

Index

A
Airedale terrier 172
Alcuin of York 50
Angles 42, 43, 45
Anglian Tower 46
Anglo-Saxons 42, 46, 47, 49, 50-52, 80, 82, 93
archaeology 17, 18, 19, 22-27, 41, 43, 55, 59, 61, 62, 71, 93, 117
Archbishop of York 66, 89, 95, 122
Aske, Robert 121-123, 133

B
Barnsley 6-7, 149, 160, 161, 172
barrows 22, 25, 27
battles
  Adwalton Moor 141
  Brunanburgh 58
  Catterick 45
  Ferrybridge 117
  Hastings 66, 70
  Marston Moor 130, 143, 145
  Seacroft Moor 140
  Stainmore 58
  Stamford Bridge 60, 65
  Towton 114, 116, 117
  Wakefield 110, 116
  Winwidfield 44, 47
Bennett, Alan 169
Bernicia 44, 45
Beverley 6-7, 80, 89, 90
Bishop of York 45
Black Death 88-92, 94, 95
black pudding 162, 165

Bradford 6-7, 148, 149, 153, 155, 158, 159, 169, 174
Brigantia 34
Brigantes 24, 30-33
Brontë sisters 169
Bronze Age 22, 23, 26, 27
burial mounds 22

C
Caratacus 30, 31
Cartimandua 30, 31
castles 74-79
cathedrals 21, 39, 46, 73, 80, 84, 85, 119
Catterick 44, 45, 167
Cawood Sword 59
Cerialis, Quintus Petillius 32, 34
chariots 25
cheese 101, 165
child labour 146, 154, 160
Clifford's Tower 76
Clitherow, Margaret 137
coal 158-161
Cobbett, William 4
collieries 158-161
Constantine, Emperor 37
Constantius I, Emperor 37
Cook, Capt. James 169
Coppergate, York 53, 55, 59, 71
Council of the North 132, 133, 139
cricket 173
Cumbria 33

Index

D
Dark Ages 41
Deira 42-45
Delius, Frederick 169
Dench, Judi 169
Denmark 42, 50
deserted medieval villages (DMVs) 92-94
dictionary 176, 177
Dissolution of the Monasteries 120-129
Doggerland 16, 17, 19
Domesday Book 69, 71
Doncaster 6-7, 39, 47, 95, 97, 149, 156, 161

E
East Anglia 16
Eboracum 32, 34-38, 42, 47
Ebrauc 42
Edinburgh 11
Edmund of Langley 105
Edward the Confessor 63, 64
English Channel 29
English Civil War 130, 138, 139-145
Eoforwic 43, 45, 46, 52
Eric Bloodaxe (Eric Haraldsson) 57, 58

F
farming 20, 88, 92, 100, 147, 151, 170, 171
Fawkes, Guy 134-137
Ferriby 1 22, 23
fish and chips 165
football 175

G
gladiators 39
God's Own County 11
Great Army 51-52

H
Hadrian, Emperor 37
Halifax 6-7, 149, 150, 151, 174
handweaving 150-151
Harold Hardrada 63-65
Harrying of the North 67-68
Hatfield Chase 44, 46
Hockney, David 169
House of Lancaster 107
House of York 107, 132
Huddersfield 6-7, 149, 153, 174, 178, 179
Hull 6-7, 38, 91, 139, 141, 149, 162, 169, 174
Humber Estuary 7
hunting 18-20, 26, 70
Hutton, Leonard 169

I
Ice Age 15
industry 146-161
Ingham, Bernard 4
Irish Sea 11
Iron Age 24, 25, 27

J
Jews, massacre of 75
Johnson, Amy 169
Jorvik 52-54, 56, 57

K
King Charles I 138, 139, 142, 145
King Edwin 45, 46, 47, 82
King Harold II 64, 66, 70
King Henry VIII 118, 119, 124, 131, 133-135
King William I 64, 66, 67, 70, 71, 77, 99

Viking Yorkshire

L
Lake Pickering 17, 19
Lancashire 10, 11, 33, 103, 104, 111, 123, 148, 152
Lancaster 102–104, 107–112, 114–117
land bridge 15
Leeds 6–7, 140, 148, 149, 153, 154, 158, 174
Lilla Howe 22
Lindisfarne 44, 47, 50
Lloyds Bank Turd 59
Local Government Act of 1974 13
Low Bentham 11

M
Meaux Abbey 90
Mercia 46, 47, 61
Mesolithic 17–19
mills 152–154
monasteries 48, 87, 99–101, 118–121, 123, 124
Moore, Henry 169
Mother Shipton 167

N
Neolithic 20–21
Normans 61, 66, 68–71, 74, 77, 82, 83, 99
North Sea 11, 16, 19, 22, 51
Northumbria 45, 46, 47, 49, 51, 57, 58, 61, 82
Norway 50, 58, 65, 67

P
Petergate, York 39
piece hall 150
pigeons 162, 166
Pilgrimage of Grace 121, 122

R
Rhubarb Triangle 165
Richard II 79
Richard Plantagenet 105, 107–109, 112, 113, 116
Richborough 29
Richmond Castle 77, 78
Ridings of Yorkshire 6–7, 12–13, 69, 149
rivers
  Aire 7, 144, 154, 179
  Foss 32
  Humber 22, 24, 51, 91
  Ouse 7, 32, 36, 59, 74
Robin Hood 96–98
Roche Abbey 126, 127, 129
rock art 26
Romans 24, 28–43, 46, 47
Rotherham 6–7, 57, 158, 161
rugby 174

S
St Margaret of York 137
Scarborough 6–7, 17, 144, 149, 179
Scotch Corner 33
Scotland 11, 8, 141, 142
Severus, Emperor 37
Shakespeare, William 79, 104
Sharman, Helen 169
Sheffield 6–7, 80, 148, 149, 156–158, 168, 175
sheep 101, 150, 170, 171, 172
Shunner Howe 22
Siege of York 142, 145
Smith, Sydney 4
stainless steel 168
standing stones 26–27

Index

Star Carr 17, 18, 26
Stonegate, York 39
steel 156, 157
Stonehenge of the North 20-21
Swarth Howe 22

T

textiles 150-155
Thornborough Henges 20, 21

V

Vale of Pickering 17
Venutius 30, 31, 33
Vikings 12, 41-57

W

Wakefield 6-7, 80, 98, 149, 161, 165, 174
Wars of the Roses 102-117, 132
Wensleydale cheese 101
Wharram Percy 93, 94
White Rose 102, 104-106
Wilberforce, William 169

Y

York 6-7, 11, 33, 35, 38, 39, 42, 43, 50-53, 59, 61, 62, 64, 65, 67, 68, 74, 79-83, 89, 92, 97, 102-104, 107-111, 113-116, 132-134, 137, 139, 142, 143, 145, 148, 149, 169
York Castle 75, 76, 79
York Minster 39, 73, 77, 80-85, 92
Yorkshire Day 180
Yorkshire pudding 162, 164
Yorkshire Ridings 6-7, 12-13, 69, 149
Yorkshire terriers 172